A
SOLDIER WITH
RAILWAYS

By the same Author

Retreat from Burma (Foulshams 1973)
Field Security (Picton Publishing 1992)

A
SOLDIER WITH
RAILWAYS

by
Lt. Col. A.A. Mains

A SOLDIER WITH RAILWAYS

© *Lieutenant Colonel A.A. Mains*
First published in 1994
Picton Publishing (Chippenham) Limited
ISBN 0 948251 70 0

Managing editor:
David Picton-Phillips BSc

Typeset from Author's discs by
Mike Kelly Phototypesetting,
Biddestone, Chippenham, Wiltshire SN14 7EA
Printed and Bound in the United Kingdom by
Picton Publishing (Chippenham) Limited
Queensbridge Cottages,
Patterdown,
Chippenham,
Wiltshire SN15 2NS
Telephone: (0249) 443430

Picton Publishing (Chippenham) Limited
CHIPPENHAM

DEDICATION

To the Indian Railwaymen of the days of the Raj.

CONTENTS

APPENDIX

POSTSCRIPT

MAPS

x

ACKNOWLEDGEMENTS

My thanks go once again to my wife, Pauline, for reading the script and for bullying me into writing what I hope is reasonable English. Thanks also to Sir Robert Reid late Chairman of British Railways for the "Foreword" and to Mr John Price of Cook's Timetables for valuable corrections and suggestions in the final Chapter.

W Foulsham & Co Ltd of Slough have very kindly allowed me to use material from my "Retreat from Burma" in Chapter V and the Railway Gazette International have permitted me to reproduce in full my article "Journey from Pakistan to India 1947" published in the Railway Gazette in 1948.

I am greatful again to Mr Price for the loan of photographs and to Mrs Berridge for permission to use illustrations from her late husband's book "Couplings to the Khyber".

FOREWORD

by

Sir Robert Reid CBE, late Chairman of British Railways.

Tony Mains has written a fascinating book about his experiences with various Railways in the Middle East, India and Burma between 1934 and his last journey back from India by rail from Basra to Calais in 1953 (His Cook's Itinerary is reproduced in all its detail).

There is a feast of reminiscences attractive to a wide circle of readers interested not only in Railways but in a way of life of a British Officer in those years.

Some examples are tales of outwitting Turkish Customs Officers, of escaping from Japanese bombs and exploding ammunition wagons. Confrontation with panic stricken Indian Police in the retreat from Rangoon. Tales of incredibly slow railway journeys in India by troop train. All of them accompanied by accurate details of locomotive and coach types, train schedules, operating problems and solutions.

This book will appeal to all "Railway Buffs" and many readers looking for accounts of life and experiences in British India, Burma and the Middle East, before, during and just after World War II.

A Soldier with Railways.

INTRODUCTION

I will confess at the outset that I am a "Rail Buff", and have been ever since I was about nine years old. I was brought up in a railway atmosphere – my paternal grandfather was the Deputy Solicitor of the London and North Western Railway. He lived at Chiswick on the Hounslow Loop of the old London and South Western Railway, and after my mother's death in 1920, my father and I moved in with him. Two of my grandfather's colleagues from Euston joined the LSWR and continued to hold their posts after the formation of the Southern Railway – Sir Herbert Walker as General Manager and Bill Bishop as Solicitor. Thanks to them, my grandfather had a 1st Class Pass valid between Waterloo and Kew Bridge; this was in addition, of course, to his Pass on the western section of the LMS south of Carlisle, one of the perquisites of a Railway pensioner.

Additionally, my grandfather could usually obtain free 1st Class tickets for himself, my unmarried aunt, who lived with us, amd myself when we went on holiday provided it was on the LMS or SR. We went to Scotland by the "Royal Scot" in its first year of operation, I think this was 1927 or 28, before in fact either the new "Royal Scot" class locomotives or the new special stock were ready; we were hauled by two "Jumbos" of Victorian vintage. There was an order of which my grandfather was ignorant that no free passes were valid for the new train, and this was not discovered until we were past Rugby. We could not be put off, as the first passenger stop was at Symington well north of the border, but I suppose that the ticket collector could have charged us. However on finding out that my grandfather was an old LNWR man we were forgiven.

I have had a lot of fun out of railway travel in a number of countries, but it was my twenty years service in the Indian Army both before and during the last War, which extended my experiences beyond Europe. These included India, Burma, Iraq, Turkey, Syria and Lebanon, and I can say that I have travelled on such famous expresses as the Blue Train, Golden Arrow, Night Ferry, P & O Express and Taurus Express; to say nothing of the Frontier Mail and Deccan Queen together as well as many other Indian named trains.

My first journey in uniform was as a cadet corporal in the Malvern College Officers Training Corps to attend summer camp at Tidworth at the end of July 1930. Our special train was drawn up in the bay platform at Great Malvern, the platform used by the LMS branch trains to Ashchurch. Our route took us through the tunnels to Ledbury, where we diverged from the Hereford main line and took the now disused single line to Gloucester joining the South Wales line at Over Junction; passing through Gloucester GWR station, we crossed the Midland Bristol line on the level to continue on the east side of this line to Hatherley Curve Junction just south of Cheltenham. A short run on the GWR Banbury branch, before our train turned south onto the Midland and South Western Junction Railway, by then a part of the GWR – a run through Swindon (Town) to Ludgershall, then a reversal to Tidworth.

At the conclusion of the camp. our rifles and bayonets were collected to be taken back to Malvern by the permanent staff, and we were allowed to disperse individually. Two special trains were were laid on, one to Paddington and the other to Waterloo; I naturally chose the latter. This train was diverted off the main line at Byfleet and ran via Virginia Water and Staines. We were diverted again at Feltham Junction onto the Hounslow Loop, and I had hopes that we might be held by signal at Chiswick so I could get off. No such thing happened and I had the chagrin of passing within hailing distance of our house, and having to take another train back from Waterloo.

About this time the question of a career loomed up. I was sixteen and had obtained my School Certificate with five credits, three of them, however, in the arts group, – English, History and Geography. My preferences were Railways, Army, a History degree at University or the Bar; my father, a Barrister, was very much against the latter, as his career had largely collapsed as a result of his absence at the Front during the Great War. He did little to influence me over the others, although I think he preferred the Army notably, the Royal Artillery. He, himself, had held a Territorial Commission in the 3rd County of London Yeomanry (Sharpshooters), but had transferred to the Royal Artillery at the outbreak of the Great War.

I very much regret that laziness played a great part in my final decision – to take up a railway career would have meant leaving School then and there, to become a Traffic Apprentice, but the Army examination did not have to be taken until I was eighteen. I had no hope for the Gunners, as mathematics and I had never agreed, so in due course I went to Sandhurst and emerged as an Officer in the Gurkha Brigade of the Indian Army. I had no connection with either the Indian Army or the country, but made my choice on the prospect of increased responsibilty in that Army and of active service on the North West Frontier.

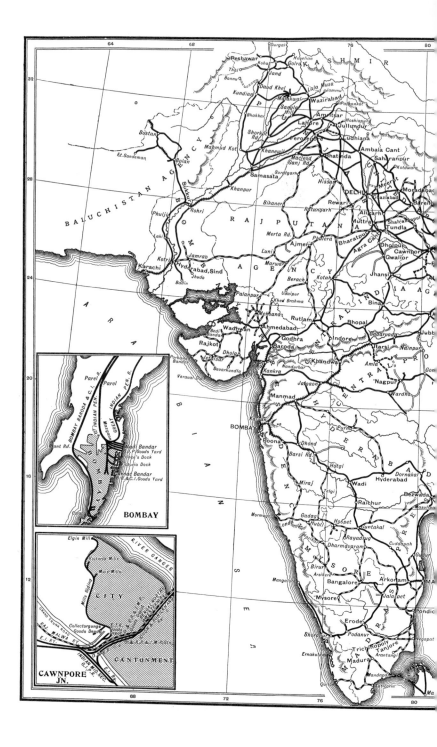

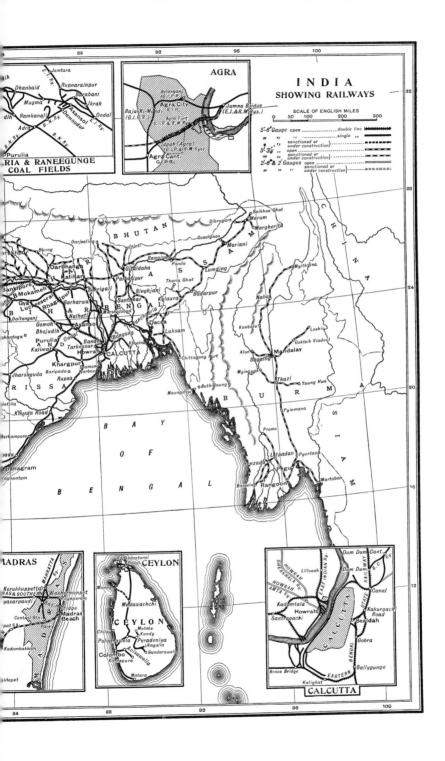

INDIA
SHOWING RAILWAYS

SCALE OF ENGLISH MILES

AGRA

BURIA & RANEEGUNGE
COAL FIELDS

MADRAS

CEYLON

CALCUTTA

PART I
INDIA 1934–40

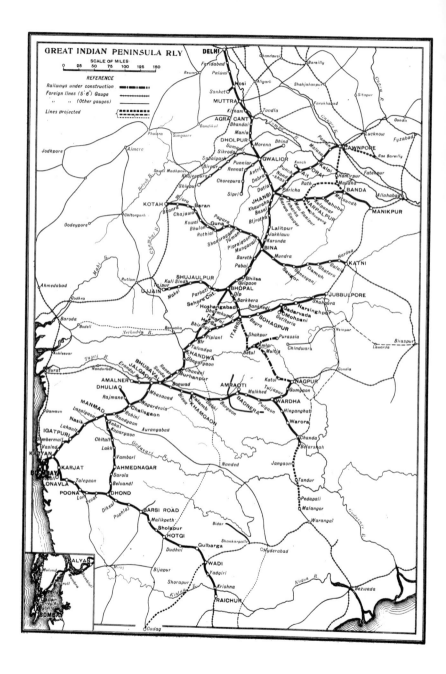

CHAPTER I – THE FIRST INDIAN JOURNEY.

My Commission into the Unattached List Indian Army (ULIA) was dated 2nd February 1934 and I was ordered to report at Southampton on 16 February to embark on the Hired Transport "Nevasa" for passage to Bombay. The *Nevasa* was a coal burning liner of 9000 tons belonging to the British India line, a subsidiary of the P & O., and on permanent charter to the War Office. Troopships on permanent charter flew the Blue Ensign and were painted white with a blue stripe and yellow funnels instead of their company livery. There was a small military permanent staff headed by a Regimental Sergeant Major and the senior Military Officer travelling was nominated O.C Troops, otherwise the command and operation of the ship was entirely in the hands of the owning company.

Soldiers travelled "troopdeck" ie in hammocks which were slung in what had been the holds; Officers, and their families in 1st Class, Warrant Officers and Sergeants 2nd Class, and soldiers families, but not the husbands, in 3rd Class. There was no difference between 1st Class on a troopship and the equivalent class on an ordinary liner – the same cabin and bath stewards, the same lavish meals with mid morning snacks or ices brought round the decks at 11 am. My only military duty was that of "Officer of the Guard"; this was assigned on a roster and involved visiting the sentries on the lifebelts two or three times during the night and reporting that all was correct to the ship's Officer of the Watch. Uniform was worn in the morning and Mess Dress for dinner.

Ours was a fast voyage stopping only at Port Said to coal; here we, the ULIAs, went ashore to Simon Artz's famous store to buy our civilan sun helmets, the well known "Bombay Bowlers". Several of us young Officers feeling that we needed some exercise arranged with the Chief Engineer for a two hour trick in the stokehold, much to the amusement of the Punjabi stokers. I was amused, when nearly twenty years later, a senior Indian Officer, later to become Chief of the Army Staff, Brigadier "Kay" Kumaramangalam, said to me "Do you remember, Tony, how we stoked the boilers of the *Nevasa* in the Red Sea?".

3

H.M. TRANSPORT "NEVASA"   *Author's Collection*
9,056 Tons.   Length 480 feet   Breadth 58.1 feet   Depth 30 feet
Sailed from Southampton Friday 16th February 1934.

About four weeks after leaving Southampton we docked at Alexandra Dock, Bombay. This was the usual dock for troopships and was situated at the southern end of the Docks close to Ballard Pier the main passenger terminal. The Embarkation Staff came on board to see to our dispersal to our various destinations. Three of us were bound for Sialkot for attachment to the 1st Battalion of the Dorset Regiment. Sialkot was located in the Punjab north west of Lahore, so we would travel on the Frontier Mail as far as Wazirabad Junction, which we would reach on the third day and there change to a local train for the final thirty miles to Sialkot. As there were a number of passengers for this train, the Bombay Baroda and Central India Railway would run a special portion of the Mail from Ballard Pier Station, and thus save us having to to join the train at Bombay Central. My servant to be, Mohammad Ishaque, who had been sent down by the Regiment, arrived on board; he relieved me of

4

my hand luggage, and my Agents, Cooks, would deal with the heavy baggage, leaving my colleagues and myself free to enjoy Bombay until 6 pm that evening.

The time soon passed and we were back at Ballard Pier Station to join our train. Ballard Pier and its Station, as well as the adjacent streets, the Ballard Estate, had been built on reclaimed land just to the north of the Naval Dockyard shortly after World War I. The Pier consisted of the jetties adjacent to the Customs Halls and the station with its four platforms. The upper floor was taken up by the Mail sorting rooms, as before the general adoption of air mails, the volume of sea mail was very large. Although the Pier was used by a number of shipping lines, the two important days were Thursdays, when the P & O Mail steamer arrived, and Saturdays when it left. On these days two trains were regular users – The Imperial Indian Mail, a luxury train of corridor vestibuled coaches with a Dining Car; practically the only train of vestibuled stock then running in India. It ran to Howrah (Calcutta) via Allahabad over the Great Indian Peninsula and East Indian Railways, the other was a portion of the Frontier Mail running to Peshawar via Delhi over the Bombay Baroda and Central India and North Western Railways.

Our special was drawn up at the platform and I had my first glimpse of an Indian passenger train. It consisted of three first and second class composites and a brake van; the coaches looked different to those I had been accustomed to in Europe, as they were considerably shorter, and, of course, wider as they were on the 5 ft 6 in gauge. Each coach, an "FSQ" in railway parlance, had only two first class coupés, each with an upper and lower transverse berth, a first class four berth with upper and lower fore and aft berths, and two second class five berth compartments together with a small compartment with hard wooden seats for servants. Ishaque was standing at the door of one of the coupés, and I found that my stable companion would be Evan Rowland Jones, who had been in the same company at Sandhurst, and was also going to Sialkot. He had been partially educated in India so his advice on rail travel was invaluble. The compartment had a leather covered lower berth and a cane bottomed chair, with the

5

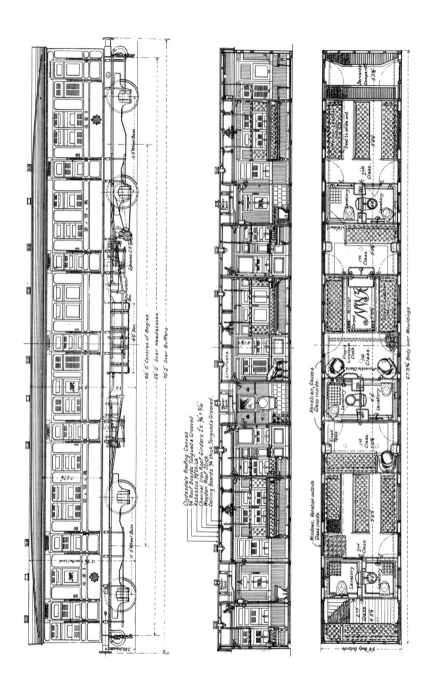

Clydesdale Roofing Canvas
¾" Roof Boards Tongued & Grooved
Asbestos 1¼" thick
Channel Iron Roof Girders 2" × ¾" × ⁵⁄₁₆"
Wooden Roof Stick
Ceiling Boards ¾" thick Tongued & Grooved

Lincrusta

Venetian, Gauze & Glass inside.

Windows, Venetian outside Glass inside.

67·9¾" Body over Mouldings

9·6" Body Outside

6

upper berth folded away. There was a small table with a mirror above fixed to the bulkhead, together with a door leading to the bathroom. This had a basin, a WC and a shower, but with cold water only and there was no form of heating. I now knew the reason for the bedding roll which the Army had provided me with as bedding was not supplied. There was, of course no corridor or vestibule as each compartment was self contained. At the head of the train was a elderly BB&CI 4–6–0 Locomotive of Class "HP" built in the Edwardian era. We were informed that the dinner stop would be at Bandra in north Bombay where we would be attached to the main portion of the Mail, which contained the Dining Car.

At about 7 pm we pulled out onto the main line of the Bombay Port Trust Railway, which we followed to the northern end of the Docks where we joined the GIP Harbour Branch, passed over the main line of that Railway to reach the BB&CI main line at Bandra. A short walk down the platform to the Dining Car, for the usual railway dinner – Soup, Fried Fish, Roast Chicken and Caramel Custard. An hour later the train stopped for us to regain our compartment. The two servants had been travelling in it, both to look after our belongings and to make up the beds. Evan initiated me into the mysteries of the three window coverings – glass, wire gauze, and wooden venetian, and explained that, however hot it might be, the venetian must be shut and bolted; as must the door as a precaution against thieves. There was no air conditioned stock at that time but all upper class compartments had electric fans and in summer an 80 lb block of ice could be placed in the compartment to help keep it cool. Conversely in certain parts of north India it was the lack of heating which was the problem when, in winter, there were hard frosts at night.

The next morning came tea and toast to our compartment and the news that breakfast would be at the next stop, Ratlam; once again we detrained and our servants took over to roll up the beds and tidy up. I went forward to have a look at the locomotive and found we now had a new Pacific, of Class "XC", for the hilly section through which we were now passing. Another departure from European practice was a driver and two firemen. as was

7

Mallet 2-6-6-2   *P.S.A. Berridge. MBE, MICE*

North Western E/M 'Atlantic' *Colonel C.F. Carson.*

P.S.A. Berridge. MBE, MICE

usual in the top links, the Driver was an Anglo Indian and the Firemen Indians. At the next stop the Engine uncoupled and went forward to coal underneath a mechanical coal stage – I believe this was the only example of this in India outside of a loco shed, and was there to avoid changing engines at Ratlam, although crews were changed. The reason was to allow the more powerful "XC" class engine to go through over the hilly part of the line, otherwise one crew one engine was normal in the Mail links. Towards afternoon engines were changed and we once again got a "HP" for the flat run to Delhi. At Muttra we left the BB&CI metals and ran the last eighty miles to Delhi by a running power over the GIP main line.

We had lunched on the train and tea had been brought to our compartment, but we arrived at Delhi too early for dinner, which was taken in the Station Refreshment Room; a similar meal to that on the train the evening before. Meanwhile our train was being remarshalled – it was usual in those days to keep the Mail trains very light partly by the exclusion of third class passengers and partly by severe distance restrictions on intermediate class (a superior type of third class). The Frontier Mail on a normal day would consist of a Postal Sorting Carriage, a Brakevan, one FSQ, and one Intermediate carriage for Peshawar; the remainder consisting of the Dining Car, two FSQs and a composite Inter and Brakevan, would come off at Delhi and be replaced by an equivalent number of North Western Railway coaches, but no Dining Car as that would be attached at Lahore on the following morning.

The Delhi stop was of about two hours so there was plenty of time to look around after dinner. There were coaches of four railways to be seen, BB&CI – yellow and brown, GIP – plum, East Indian – green and North Western – red. We left about 9 pm behind another elderly locomotive a North Western "E1" class Atlantic which would take us to Lahore; there, the next morning, we acquired a Dining Car in time for breakfast and two class "SP" 4–4–0s as motive power. We reached Wazirabad Junction at midday and changed into the branch train of somewhat elderly and decrepit coaches hauled by a goods Engine, a class "SG" 0–6–0,

9

the maid of all work on Indian Railways

We arrived at Sialkot at lunch time and so ended my first journey – a distance of about 1000 miles which had taken some 42 hours.

Pakistan Western Railway "SG Class" 0-6-0.

John Price

CHAPTER II – THE RAILWAYS OF THE RAJ.

I did a considerable amount of rail travel between my arrival in India in 1934 and my departure for overseas service in 1941, but to understand my journeys it is necessary for me to say a few words about the Railways in India – "The Railways of the Raj".

The first line was opened from Bombay to Thana in 1853 as part of the Great Indian Peninsula system, and, only a year later, the first train left Calcutta (Howrah Station) on the East Indian Railway. From these small beginnings a network was built up which by 1934, excluding Burma, consisted of over 43,000 route miles, the third largest in the world. These lines were worked by 42 different operating agencies, although only the nine broad gauge railways and about three of the metre gauge lines were of any size or importance. A number of the others were metre gauge lines owned and worked by Indian Native States or narrow gauge (2 ft 6 or 2ft) lines of private companies.

The original lines were built to the gauge of 5 ft 6, a gauge which is found elsewhere only in Ceylon, the Iberian Peninsula, Argentina and Chile. These lines, linking the major cities for strategic reasons, were built by Companies incorporated in England, and under contract to the Government of India, who guaranteed 5% on the capital invested and in most cases provided free land. All the major cities of India had been linked by the seventies, but the scandal caused by the mismanagement and waste on these early lines caused the Government in the eighties to buy out all the original companies. Nationalisation was a dirty word, however, in Victorian times, so with the exception of the North Western for strategic reasons, and the East Bengal and the Oudh and Rohillakund which were bankrupt, all the lines bought out were handed back to the private companies to operate on behalf of the Government. At the same time private companies were encouraged to build and operate metre gauge lines, without any guarantee, but with free land and an option allowing the Government to determine the contract after a period of years.

This policy led to a somewhat bizarre situation whereby, in

1922, the the Government owned 73% of the lines, the Indian Native States 12% and only 15% was privately owned. Conversely the private companies and the Native States worked 79% of the lines to the Government's 21%. The Government in the same year decided that, with the exception of a few narrow gauge light railways, all lines in British India, as distinct from the Native States, should be owned and managed by the State. It was decided further, that instead of direct and immediate nationalisation, the lines should be taken over as and when their respective operating contracts expired. The first companies, taken over in 1925, were the GIP and the East Indian, who thus joined the North Western and Eastern Bengal as State Railways; the State operated Oudh and Rohillakund was amalgamated with the East Indian. The remaining broad gauge lines – the BB & CI, the Bengal Nagpur, the Madras and Southern Mahratta and the South Indian – were still company operated when I arrived in India in 1934, and the final broad gauge railway – His Exalted Highness the Nizam's State Railway was owned and operated by the Indian State of Hyderabad. All the metre gauge lines, with the exception of the East Bengal's metre gauge component, were operated by, but not necessarily owned by, private companies or Native States.

The metre gauge network was very extensive as it comprised over 40% of the total mileage, but, except for the extreme north east and extreme south, it did not serve any major city or port. It served the southern part of the Madras Presidency, Rajputana and Kathiawar, the northern part of the United Provinces, Bihar, and Bengal together with the Province of Assam.

Passenger train services were neither very frequent nor very fast. The norm was a "Mail", an "Express" and a "Passenger" on each of the main lines. The Mail was a very light train, usually carrying only 1st and 2nd class passengers, although some trains admitted Intermediate class but only for the whole run. The Express was a heavy train running at a much lower speed and carried 1st, 2nd, Inter and 3rd class and the Passenger, carrying all four classes, normally stopped at all stations. The Frontier Mail, India's premier long distance train, averaged 36 mph over

12

the 860 miles between Bombay and Delhi, and this was typical of most Mail trains. Broad Gauge Passengers averaged rather over 20 mph. The metre gauge Delhi Mail averaged 25 mph over the 580 miles between Ahmadabad and Delhi. These speeds included stops which were largely responsible for the low overall speeds. No Mail train ran for over two hours without a stop, and station stops were seldom less than ten minutes or longer if engines or crews had to be changed. These long stops were necessitated by the need to serve meals to passengers and to replenish the carriage roof tanks; this was a most time consuming business as each upper class carriage had a tank to each lavatory, and a lavatory to each compartment, and often this was accomplished by the watercarrier walking along the roof with his skin waterbag. Another factor was the prevalence of single lines with the usual hazard of bad crossings.

I have described a typical 1st & 2nd Class carriage in Chapter I; Inter and 3rd Class travelled in considerable discomfort in crowded accomodation with hard seats. Only three trains had corridor or vestibuled stock, the Imperial Indian Mail, already mentioned, and two daytime only trains – the Deccan Queen and the Assam Mail, but for 1st and 2nd class passengers only. Meals were provided for Upper Class passengers either by a trip to the Restaurant Car at a convenient stop or by the provision of meals from station restaurants which were served in the compartments. At this time there were only ten Broad Gauge and three Metre Gauge trains provided with Restaurant Cars. The most important member of the train staff for the passengers was the Conductor who dealt with the reservations and berthing of upper class passengers. One of his main duties was their feeding – seeing that the train stopped at convenient stations for passengers to enter and leave the Restaurant Car, or to send telegrams to the appropriate stations for meals to be made ready, when this facility was non existent. He was responsible, also, in the hot weather for the provision of ice and ice containers.

There was no Air Conditioned stock at this time and the only way of cooling a compartment was by an ice container with an 80lb block of ice placed on the floor of the compartment; with the

13

fan playing on it, it caused the temperature to drop several degrees. The first air conditioned coaches made their appearance in early 1936 on the Frontier Mail as a joint venture of the North Western and BB & CI Railways; the service was later extended to the North Western's Karachi Mail. The cooling agent was 80 lb blocks of ice carried in a container under the centre of the an ordinary upper class coach, and replenished at intervals during the journey; only the three centre 1st class compartments were converted, with the 2nd class compartments at the end left as they were. Places in these coaches were always fully booked but there was a disadvantage; should the train be delayed so that the ice had melted before the rebunkering stop was reached, the compartments became infernos as the windows were sealed and double glazed and the system merely blew in hot air. The following year the GIP constructed a modern electro-mechanical air conditioned coach in their Bombay workshops. The interior layout followed that of the coaches of the Imperial Indian Mail – two and four berth corridor compartments. It was vestibuled at one end only – so that it would be coupled to a Restaurant Car, but this was in the future as no Car running at that time was vestibuled. In fact the standard layout of Restaurant Cars was a Saloon in the centre and at one end the kitchen, crews' quarters and an Indian type latrine, and at the other end, cabins for the Manager, and the train Conductor together with a European type lavatory.

The light make up of the Mail trains was due to the age and lack of power of the locomotive stock. India, with a few exceptions, had never manufactured locomotives; she had bought what was on offer from the various builders in Britain. The purchase of the main line companies caused the Government to consider some measure of standardisation, and at the turn of the century on the advice of their Consultant Engineers, Messrs Rendel, Palmer & Tritton, decided to purchase the British Engineering Standards Association (BESA) locomotives. These were the "HP" Class 4–6–0 for passenger trains and the "HG" 2–8–0 for goods. They joined the non standard "E1" Class Atlantics and "SP" Class 4–4–0s for passenger work and the

14

ubiquitous 0–6–0s of Class "SG" for goods traffic. All of these Classes had narrow fireboxes within the driving wheels and were designed to burn high quality imported coal. With the exception of such Indian features as the headlight, cowcatcher, and tender cab, they would not have looked out of place on any British railway. By 1934 many of these locomotives had been rebuilt with superheaters; they were distinguished by the suffix "S" ie "HPS" or "SGS". I have ommitted this for clarity in describing locomotives.

The Indian Railways were severely affected by World War I, and to quote from a Railway Board Report, ended it in a "battered and dilapidated condition". One of the most urgent needs was the replacement of the ageing locomotives, many of which were in poor condition due to lack of maintenance during the War. Unfortunately much time was lost in determining which types would be the most suitable for Indian conditions. A pre-condition was that the new engines should be able to use the cheap low quality Indian coal, and this would mean a Pacific type with a wide firebox, which in its turn posed the question as to whether these heavier machines would be able to run safely on the existing track. By the time all this had been resolved and the first orders placed, the world wide depression had set in and shortage of money prevented further purchases. Thus few of the new locomotives had been received by 1934.

The major Classes on the Broad gauge, all Pacifics, were the "XA" for light branch line track, the "XB" for heavy main line expresses and the "XC" for Mail trains. A metre gauge Pacific, the "YB", had also appeared but it was subject to severe restrictions as to the lines it was able to run.

There were two electrified main lines, the GIP main lines up the Ghats, that is the escarpment between the coastal plain and the Deccan plateau – 120 miles Bombay to Poona on the south east main line and 83 miles to Igatapuri on the north east. The ruling gradient was 1 in 37, and before electrification trains had to be divided and taken up through reversing stations by special tank engines; now trains could go up as one and the reversing stations were no longer necessary, but all trains still had to be

15

Cabin lever frame provided at cabin interlocked stations on the Indian Railways.

banked up the worst sections. The system was overhead wires at 1500 Volts dc, and the locomotives, built in Britain by Metropolitan Vickers were 1–D-1 machines for passenger work and coupled 0–6–0+0–6–0s with central cabs for goods trains and bankers.

India followed British practice in signalling; all double and single lines were worked on the absolute block with block and token instruments of British pattern. Some Indian practices were somewhat old fashioned and dated from before the introduction of continuous brakes. Because of the general low standard of education, there was no grade of Signalman, so the block working was carried out by Assistant Station Masters with the instruments in the station building and not in the signal cabin. The cabins, whose levers were slotted from the ASM's office, were manned by pointsmen, whose sole function was to pull over levers as required by the ASM. The rules required the duty ASM to display a green flag or lamp to the crew of any train "running through". Sidelights were still used on passenger brakevans, and front guards carried on all Mail and Express trains. The Fireman and Front Guard were required to look out and exchange signals with the Head Guard until they were satisfied that the whole of their train was safely moving out of a station.

The senior railway Officers were mostly Europeans, but the remainder of the staff were Indians, except for a sizeable minority of Anglo-Indians. They were either the descendents of the original hands who had come out in the early days from Britain or were time expired British soldiers who had taken their discharge in India. They were found as Drivers and Firemen in the top links and as Foremen in the Railway Workshops – a few were Stationmasters of the more important stations and the Conductors on Mail trains were invariably Anglo-Indians.

XC Pacific on Mail Train.   *P.S.A. Berridge. MBE, MICE*

P.S.A. Berridge. MBE, MICE

Punjab Mail G.I.P. 4-6-0 loco.

'XC' Clan Pacific on Karachi Mail.   *P.S.A. Berridge. MBE, MICE*

Metro Vick 0-6-0 "+" 0-6-0 electric locomotive.   *John Price*

CHAPTER III

INDIA, PRE WAR JOURNEYS – 1934–40

I have called this Chapter "Pre War Journeys" but in fact it continues up to April 1941, when I was posted to Iraq. My reason is that up to this time, the passenger services on Indian Railways had not been affected by the War.

I made a considerable number of journeys during this period, but except for one metre gauge trip to Belgaum south of Bombay, all were in the north west; in fact on the North Western, BB & CI, GIP, and the north western part of the East Indian, as well as on the metre gauge Jodhpur Railway. I quickly found out that most Anglo Indian drivers would give you a ride on the footplate if asked, so I was able to ride on the engines of the Frontier Mail, the GIP's Punjab Mail, the metre gauge Poona-Bangalore Mail, as well as a number of other trains.

The hill station to which the Dorsets went in the hot weather, was Solan on the 2ft 6 gauge Hill railway, which enabled me to to see this very interesting line as well as the stock in which British troops travelled on the broad gauge. The normal arrangement was that the Regimental Headquarters, the families, and two of the four companies went up to the "hills" in mid April, and these two companies changed over with the two left in Sialkot in mid July, and they, with the Headquarters and the families came down in early October. My company was in the second party.

The special train provided consisted of two four wheeled 1st and 2nd Class coaches for Officers, Warrant Officers and Sergeants, a number of "Military Cars" for the soldiers, two four wheeled covered goods wagons for baggage and a four wheeled brake van. The Military Cars were owned by the Defence Department and distributed to the various Railways for use on troop trains as required. The reason was that the medical authorities would not allow British soldiers to travel in 3rd Class, with its lack of fans and other amenities, and to carry a battalion, or even a company, in 2nd class coaches would have entailed the provision of far too much stock. These Cars, known as "M"s, were painted in a dirty

21

shade of green, and were corridor with end doors and vestibuled. They consisted of six berth couchette type compartments; these without doors and the partitions were of open steel work rather like an American Jail. Lavatories and drinking water faucets wee provided at each end. On long journeys they could be vestibuled to an "MK", a military kitchen car, staffed by a British Warrant Officer and Indian civilian cooks. Meals could be collected by the soldiers in their Mess Tins without the necessity of a stop.

Our journey was a relatively short one, so no Kitchen car was provided – instead the evening meal was to be provided by a civilian contractor at Amritsar and breakfast the next morning at Kalka, where the transhipment to the narrow gauge would be made. Our route was by branch lines by- passing Lahore to gain the main line at Amritsar, thence to Amballa, where we would reverse to go up to the broad gauge railhead at Kalka. As I was the juniormost Officer I got the majority of the duties. I had to oversee the loading of the baggage – no sinecure when the wagon was an all steel one and the temperature was over 100°F; I had to take my turn also as duty Officer, travelling in the troops' cars when the train was running and, in particular, to see that the armed sentries on the doors were alert. They were required to detrain and take up an alert position whenever the train stopped, whether at a station or not, and to jump on again as soon as it restarted. We reached Amritsar at about 7 pm for the long meal halt; while the soldiers were feeding, the Officers had dinner in the 1st Class Refreshment Room. Afterwards I was sent to get the "No Looting" certificate from the duty Assistant Station Master. This was required at each long halt as without it, the local Officials would charge every loss or breakage on the station for the last month or so to the unit concerned.

After breakfast at Kalka, we started transhipping personnel and baggage into two waiting narrow gauge trains. The Kalka-Simla Railway had been built by a private company and opened in 1903; it was bought out two years later and handed over to the North Western to operate. It is a switchback rising from 2,400 ft at Kalka to a summit of 5,200 ft at mile 23, then a drop down through Solan to 4,600 ft before the final climb to arrive at Simla at 6,800 ft. This altitude compares with the 7,400 summit of the Darjeeling

22

Himalayan and the 7,200 summit of the North Western's narrow gauge Zhob Valley line in Baluchistan. The line is just under 60 miles long and has a ruling gradient of 1 in 37; it is extremely tortuous following the sides of valleys and often tunnelling through the spurs, there are 106 tunnels in all, and crossing the re-entrants on multi arch bridges, the same construction as can be seen on Roman aqueducts in southern Europe. The longest stretch of straight track is less than three quarters of a mile and that in the Barog Tunnel.

The construction and operation was of a very high standard for a narrow gauge railway; the track is single and laid with 60 lb rails and divided into nineteen block and crossing stations, giving an average block section of three miles, each equipped with the North Western's type of single line token apparatus and with wire locked signals and points. The motive power, introduced before World War I. were the "K" Class 2–6–2T tank locomotives, specially built by the North British Locomotive Company. They had a number of unusual features – as they were never turned, the coal bunker was on each side of the boiler forward of the cab, and headlights were mounted front and back. The engines had a curious box like appearance as the combined coalbunkers, and side water tanks completely hid the boiler and smokebox, with only the chimney and top of the dome protruding. They were extremely successful and lasted until dieselisation well after Indedendence; in fact the Standardisation Committee's recommendation for this type, the "ZF" Class, was only a slightly modified version of the "K" Class with a higher tractive rating.

To speed up 1st Class and mail traffic, the North Western built a number of petrol driven railcars, at first four wheeled, but later carried on two four wheeled bogies. Except for a conventional diesel powered car, put into service in 1934, they bore a strong resemblance to the char-a-bancs, then running on the roads – transverse seats with a door to each row, with the rear row reserved for mail bags and postal staff. The driver sat on the right of the front row with passengers on his left, and, except for a hand brake wheel where the steering wheel would have been, the controls were those of a motor vehicle. The headlight mounted on the bonnet, was pivoted and linked to the front bogie so that the light could follow an approaching curve. The railcars could only be driven from one end so turntables had to be provided at Kalka and Simla.

The Cantonment at Solan was almost encircled by the railway, which also tunnelled under the ridge on which it was built; this gave plenty of opportunity for observing the trains. I am afraid that my friends and I were in the habit of walking through the tunnel when no train was due, keeping a wary eye for an specials which might appear, when we would dive into one of the refuge recesses.

The only other journey that I undertook in my first year was to Dehra Dun to join my Gurkha Regiment, the 2/9th Gurkhas. I took the branch train to Wazirabad and then on to Lahore by the Frontier Mail. My onward journey was not by the through train, the Dehra Dun Passenger, but by a through coach which left several hours later on the Calcutta Mail and was worked up the Dehra Dun branch by the Delhi-Dehra Dun Express, arriving three hours before the Passenger. The part of the Dehra line onwards from the holy city of Hardwar had been built by an Indian private company, the Hardwar-Dehra Railway Company, but worked by the East Indian. It was quite a scenic route, with a ruling gradient of 1 in 75 – at first alongside the River Ganges and then climbing through the forests of the Doon Valley with the first range of the Himalayas in view to the north.

I decided to take my two months "Privilege Leave" in 1936 ex India, and to return home as my father's health was far from good and I would not have been due for "Long Leave" until the following year at the earliest. This was quite possible as, by taking casual leave (as was allowed) to get to and from Bombay, five weeks less two days could be spent in England, using the P & O's scheduled services and going overland from Marseilles. I had to travel cheaply as I was not entitled to use one of my free passages on short leave, but I found that the P & O were running an extra boat, the *Moldavia*; she had been demoted from the mail run and was doing a one class 2nd Class run from Australia with the fare linked to the type of cabin. To clear cabins for the popular Riviera-England sea trip, the P & O gave a free overland rail ticket of the same class as the steamer ticket.

24

My route to Bombay was by the overnight Delhi Express from Dehra, breakfast at Delhi and the Frontier Mail onwards. The *Moldavia* was scheduled to leave on the same day as the mail boat so the BB & CI laid on a portion to Ballard Pier. I remember that, after dinner, I had a footplate trip from Ratlam to the next stop. I was fascinated to see the way the young Anglo Indian first fireman exchanged the tablets. Hand exchange with a net into which the old tablet was thrown, was quite usual in India, and this was so on the BB & CI, even with speeds of fifty mph. The fireman would draw a padded sock over his forearm; the headlight would be illuminating the net and the pointsman, who stood in a sort of pulpit, holding up with one hand the stick to which the ring of the tablet pouch was attached, and a flaming torch with the other. The old tablet went out first into the net and then the new tablet was picked up, the pouch and the stick hitting the tender with a resounding bang; some drivers had the tender side padded to avoid damage to the paintwork, they probably considered this more important than the fireman's arm.

I could not afford the P & O Express from Marseilles, even if the *Moldavia* had connected with it, which it did not, so I caught an ordinary Rapide, travelling overnight to Paris 2nd Class. The train, which should have arrived in ample time to catch the midday English service from the Gare de Nord, was very late, but thanks to a hair raising taxi drive across Paris, I reached the station with only minutes in hand. To my great joy one of the coaches at the rear of my train was a 2nd Class Pullman, and there was room; uttering a sigh of relief, I stumbled into it just as the train started and was soon eating a superb lunch. My return was by the weekly mail boat and my father very kindly paid the Wagon Lits supplement for me to return by the P & O Express.

The P & O Express was one of the "Grands Express" or "Trains de Luxe" composed entirely of stock belonging to the "Compagnie Internationale des Wagons Lits et des Grands Express Europeens" – Sleeping and Restaurant cars with special Luggage Vans (fourgons). It was one of the oldest of the Grands Express and, further, it was the second of such trains to receive after World War I, the new British built all steel blue sleeping cars of Class "LX", which were to replace the older wooden carriages. The first train to receive such stock was the Calais Mediteranean Express in 1922, and thus it became known as the "Blue Train". The desire to speed up the Indian mail boats in the later part of the nineteenth century caused the P & O steamers to call at Brindisi, with a special postal train running from Calais, and in 1889, a number of sleeping cars were attached to it. The following year a new special train the "Brindisi Peninsula & Oriental Express" was run. The P & O mail boats started to call at Marseilles in the same year and to cater for them, a new train, the "Bombay Express" was put on, the Brindisi train becoming the "Peninsula Express". With the exception of a short period in 1914–15, the former train survived World War I, and by 1936 had become known officially as the "P & O Express" with the company's badge of a rising sun on its name boards. It ran from Calais to Marseilles docks once a week in each direction, with a connection from London.

The train from London, consisting of Pullman cars only, left Victoria at 1.50 pm on Thursdays, ten minutes ahead of the ordinary afternoon service to Paris – the P & O passengers travelling on the ordinary afternoon boat from Dover to Calais. In actual fact, in the summer when travellers were few, two reserved Pullmans on the ordinary 2 pm train sufficed. The Express, consisting usually of six sleeping cars, a restaurant car, and two fourgons left Calais at 5.45 pm, and travelling round the Ceinture reached the Gare de Lyon after dinner; it finally arrived at Marseilles at 10.45 am on the following morning. The Bombay bound steamer awaiting the special postal train from England did not leave until midnight, but as the steamer from Bombay had already arrived the same stock made up the return train, which left at 4.52 pm arriving at Victoria at 3.30 pm on Saturdays.

My return journey was especially memorable as King Fuad of Egypt having just died, the new King, Farouk – a Cadet at the Royal Military Academy had to return home in a hurry. The British Government arranged a special train to Dover and a destroyer to take him to Calais. He, and his suite, then joined the P & O Express, travelling in the three carriages forward of the restaurant car, while we, the ordinary passengers, travelled in the rear. There was a grand reception at the Gare de Lyon, with a Guard of Honour and the Band of the Garde Republicaine during our forty minutes stop. I travelled both ways on this train on "long leave" in the following year; as the Government was paying my fare and, owing to the death of my father, I was not short of cash, I occupied a 1st Class single berth compartment. The French Railways put on a new train in 1939, the "Train Aerodynamique", the predecessor of the post war "Mistral". This left Paris at midday and arrived at Marseilles (St Charles) at 9 pm, in plenty of time to catch the boat which did not leave before midnight. It was possible to leave London by the Night Ferry as late as 10 pm on the previous evening, change trains and stations in Paris and still arrive in time. The new train did the trip at an average speed of 60 mph and was two hours faster than the morning Rapide. New air smoothed stock had been built, but, when I travelled, the look was spoiled by an old square ended fourgon between the locomotive and the train.

In September 1936, I was ordered to attend the Course for Regimental Signal Officers at Poona. Poona is situated on the GIP's south east main line at a distance of 120 miles from Bombay; this line leaves the north east main line, that to Delhi and Calcutta, at Kalyan Junction forty miles out from Bombay. As I was passing so near to Bombay, I decided to take two or three days leave to stay with some friends of my family. The shortest route would have been by the Frontier Mail to Bombay, and then onwards at the conclusion of my leave. Red tape then stepped in; this would mean two tickets and the journey would be part duty and part leave causing confusion as to which part the Government would pay for. I was told that I must have a through ticket to Poona by the shortest route, that was via Delhi and Kalyan, but that I continue in the train up to Bombay, and pay the Travelling Ticket Examiner to excess my ticket for travel from Kalyan to Bombay and back. This was the first time that I had travelled by the GIP's Punjab Mail, which left one hour before the Frontier Mail but arrived at Bombay some three hours later. I was amused to see that when we arrived at Muttra, a brow was let down and a procession of coolies rushed across, each flinging a basket of coal into the tender. The reason was that the GIP had no Shed at Delhi so their engines went to the North Western's Shed, and taking coal there sould have caused accounting problems; the extra fuel was taken on to allow engines to get back to their home Shed at Jhansi. The GIP's mail engines were the BESA 4–6–0s, but after rebuilding in the railway's workshops at Bombay, they emerged with new class letters such as – "D3", "D3M" and "D4".

Delhi was not at the turn of the century a great commercial centre, nor was it the Capital until 1911, so the first broad gauge direct line from Bombay, that of the GIP, did not reach there until 1902; the BB&CI line was even later arriving in 1909. Up to that time the only direct route was by the BB & CI, via Ahmadabad, with a break of gauge there. The GIP's Mail ran via Agra, Gwalior, Bhopal and Itarsi to Igatapuri, where the change was made to electric traction for the descent of the Ghats. The original line from Agra to Itarsi had been constructed by a private company, the Indian Midland, but worked by the GIP; it was bought out in 1900, when it was formally merged with the latter. The Government of India, however did not own the whole route. A portion south of Gwalior was owned by the Maharaja of Gwalior, and further south the Bhopal-Itarsi section was the property of the Nawab of Bhopal. Much the same occured on the rival BB & CI route – the State of Jaipur owned those sections of the Ratlam-Muttra line which lay within the State's territory. The Punjab Mail entered Bombay by coming down the scenic "Ghat" section with its tunnels, viaducts and 1 in 37 gradients, unlike the Frontier Mail which followed the coastline on the flat.

On the conclusion of my leave, I went up to Poona by the electric hauled Deccan Queen, India's fastest and most comfortable train. I was to travel on it several times when taking a day's leave in Bombay. 1st and 2nd Class only, corridored and vestibuled, with a Restaurant Car, it left Poona at 7.45 am each morning. with breakfast served en route, and arrived at Bombay at 11 am. In the evening the departure was at 5.45 pm arriving at Poona at 9 pm, after dinner had been served. The actual overall speed was only 38 mph, but this was conditioned by the very low speeds up and down the 28 mile "ghat" section with its 1 in 37 gradients, together with the additional stops to attach and detach the banker. On the level an average speed of 46 mph was attained, considerably faster than any other train in India.

The following year saw me coming south again by the Punjab Mail as far as Kalyan; this time I was to attend an "Anti Gas Course" at Belgaum, which was situated on the Madras and Southern Mahratta's metre gauge Poona-Bangalore main line; this was the furthest south that I ever travelled by rail during my service. The M & SM, still company operated, was formed by a forced marriage between the broad gauage Madras Railway and the metre gauge Southern Mahratta, when the Government bought out the former in 1908. The original conception of the Southern Mahratta was a west to east railway from Goa on the Indian Ocean to Masulapatam on the Bay of Bengal; it was odd that the Government of India did not own the two extremities – the fifty miles from Goa were built and owned by a British company, the West of India Portuguese Railway Co Ltd, under a concession from the Government of Portugal, while the eastern end was owned by the District Board (County Council) of the District of Kistna. On my way back, I went forward, when engines were being changed at Belgaum and found a new "YB" Pacific backing on; a word with the Anglo Indian driver and I was on the footplate for a ride to the next stop.

Two very interesting trips came my way in 1939; we were due for a move to the Khyber Pass during the winter of 1939–40, so the C.O. sent me with two Gurkha Officers and two senior N.C.Os to spy out the land. The Government did not pay "Mail" fares for N.C.Os so we travelled on a Passenger train stopping at all stations and taking two nights en route. There was little discomfort in this, as the Guard wired ahead for my meals, which were brought to the compartment at convenient halts, and the Gurkhas bought their food from the platform vendors. On our return to Dehra Dun we found all in confusion; the Battalion was to move to Nowshera in four days time to replace the British Battalion who had been rushed off to the Middle East as soon as war had broken out.

On this occasion instead of being the dogsbody, I was O.C. Train and also acting Commandant of the Battalion. Our move took place in early September before Officers on long leave had returned; we had present three Field Officers, no Captains and five Subalterns,

29

of which I, with only five years service, was the senior. The C.O. was being posted out, one Major had already left with the advance party, and the other was remaining as O.C. Depot, so I became the acting Commandant. My main headeache this time was not the "No Looting" certificate but the taking over of the train. Indian and Gurkha soldiers travelled in ordinary 3rd class carriages, and the railway administration usually managed to provide the oldest and most decrepit stock that they could find. Every defect had to be noted down and the defect sheet signed by the Stationmaster at the departure station, otherwise the Battalion would be charged for them on arrival. I do not remember much of the actual journey which took about 36 hours, except for one incident. I had read in a book, by an Indian Railway Officer, Victor Bailey, how in the hot weather, he had had his saloon placed under a water crane and the water turned on. We arrived very hot for a long halt at Lahore, and prevailed on the Stationmaster to turn on the carriage watering taps above our carriage; this cooled it down considerably.

The Battalion moved to its original destination at Landi Kotal at the head of the Khyber Pass in November. This involved travelling up the strategic Khyber Railway. The idea of a railway through the Khyber Pass dated back to the 2nd Afghan War of 1878, but had been repeatedly shelved on account of expense and the difficulty of finding a suitable route. The Government, however, frightened by the 3rd Afghan War of 1919, ordered a new survey and this showed that, with heavy construction costs and the use of reversing stations, a line could be built which would allow the use of the standard HG 2–8–0s as motive power. The ruling gradient up to Landi Kotal is 1 in 33 with two reversing stations, followed by a drop to Landi Khana close to the frontier at 1 in 25. The line is not particularily scenic and the main interest is in the difficulties of construction – thirty two tunnels and ninety two bridges and culverts in about thirty miles. My task in the move was the loading of our thirty six mules; these animals had been marched down from Landi Kotal to Nowshera, and had been on the Frontier all their working lives. They had never been trained to enter railway wagons and the task of getting ten untrained mules to enter and remain in an ordinary steel goods wagon – five a side, heads towards the centre

30

with only a rope to tether them was a daunting task. We were lucky that no one was hurt in the fracas that occurred.

I made no journeys by rail in 1940, but in January 1941 I received a posting order to join as an Instructor, the new Intelligence School being formed at Bombay. My route was direct from Peshawar by the Frontier Mail; we had the usual hotch-potch of locomotives – an "XA" light Pacific to Rawalpindi, two "SP" 4–4–0s to Lahore and then an "E1" Atlantic to Delhi- the BB & CI came up with an "HP" 4–6–0 to Gangapur City, followed by a "XC" Pacific to Baroda with another "HP" for the final run down the coast to Bombay. Bombay (military) Headquarters, to whom I reported, told me that no Intelligence School was being formed at Bombay – telephone calls and signals to Army Hadquarters finally located the School at Karachi.

The usual way for military, and indeed any passengers, to travel there from Bombay was by sea, as this took no longer and was cheaper than the detour by rail. The War, however, had put paid to regular coastal services so to my great joy I set off by train. This involved travel over the lines of three administrations and two changes on account of break of gauge. I was lucky that all my meals over the forty hour journey could be taken in Restaurant Cars. My journey started in the evening by the BB & CI's Gujarat Mail, arriving at Ahmadabad the next morning, where I changed into the same company's metre gauge Delhi Mail; I had hoped for a new "YB" Pacific, but was unlucky as what backed on was an "H" Class 4–6–0, the metre gauge version of the "HP". Breakfast was taken in the Restaurant Car, and I was intrigued to find that this car had a 1st Class compartment at the one end with a communicating door. This would have been no use to me as I had to travel in the through coach for Hyderabad (Sind). Lunch followed later and about tea time we reached Marwar Junction where my coach was cut off and coupled to the Jodhpur Railway's Marwar Mail for the short run to Luni Junction; there the same Railway's Sind Mail, Jodhpur to Hyderabad, was waiting. My coach was attached to this train and after I had boarded the Jodhpur Railway's Restaurant Car, we started off for the run across the Thar or Indian Desert.

The line had been built, and was owned, by the Government of India, who had made an agreement with the Maharaja of Jodhpur that the whole line should be stocked and worked as an integral part of the Jodhpur Railway. This caused trouble at Partition as the Jodhpur Government, while agreeing that the part of the line within Sind, was now owned by Pakistan, maintained that the whole of the stock was their property. The dispute rumbled on until the summer of 1948, when the Pakistanis cut the line and brought to an end the last cross border services in the West. I noticed the next morning that, contrary to normal practice, the line clear tablets were exchanged with the Guard instead of with the engine crew. Hyderabad was reached in mid morning, and shortly afterwards the North Western's broad gauge Bolan Mail steamed in – the XC Pacific looking immense after the metre gauge 4–6–0s. Lunch in the Restaurant Car followed and an arrival at Karachi in late afternoon.

Little did I think that I would be travelling back to Bombay by the same route within two months under posting to Iraq. A chapter of my Indian journeys then came to an end.

No. 1 up Mail nearing Simla.   *P.S.A. Berridge. MBE, MICE*

Kalka Station. KS Railway. Diesel Railcar on left.

Simla Station. Built on arches from hillside. Height 5600 feet.
P.S.A. Berridge. MBE, MICE

Kafir Tanga Tunnel in the Khyber Pass.

Simla Railway Station.

Petrol Rail Car. KS Railway.

Metro Gauge 'H' Class 4–6–0.

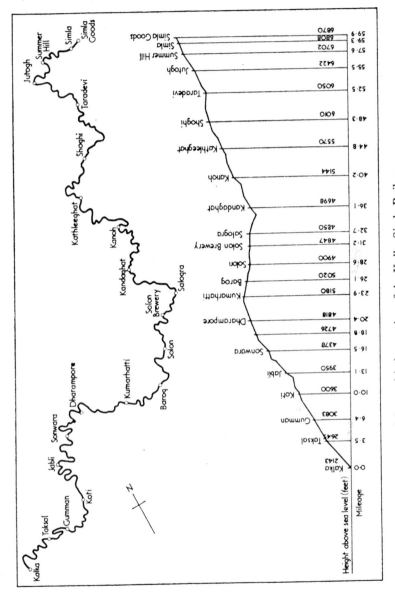

Map and index section of the Kalka Simla Railway.

PART II

WAR – IRAQ, BURMA, EASTERN INDIA – 1941–44

Running through wild country and mountains of Turkey. The Taurus Express.

Photo: R. Hodson

CHAPTER IV

PASSPORTS ON THE "TAURUS" – 1941.

I was appointed a General Staff Officer 3rd Grade (Intelligence) (GSO III (I)) in Headquarters Iraq Force, and, by a co-incidence, sailed from Bombay on the same troopship, the "Nevasa", which had brought me to India in 1934. On our arrival in Basra, we were caught up in what became known as the "Raschid Ali rebellion", as well as the floods which cut Basra off from the rest of the country. My first journey, therefore, was on a troop train to Baghdad a month or so after we had landed, and on arrival there I was appointed to head the Security or (b) section of Intelligence.

The Iraq Railways comprised two distinct entities – the metre gauge in the south and east and the standard gauge to the north of Baghdad. The metre gauge had its inception in the lines constructed by the British Forces in World War I. The main line was from Baghdad (West) to Basra with two short branches. Basra, the old port of Sinbad the Sailor, was now three miles inland, and a new town named Ashar had grown up on the river bank; this was the Port used by the British during the Mespotamian campaign. There were no jetties and ships discharged into lighters. Later under the energetic management of Colonel Sir John Ward, an R.E. Officer appointed Director of Ports and Railways, rail served jetties were constructed at Maq'il, or Margil as it was more usually known, two or three miles upstream of Ashar. Here a town on the lines of an Indian cantonment was laid out, together with the railway station, an airfield, moorings for flying boats and a hotel; a vital staging point for the air services from Europe to the Far East and Australia. The eastern section's terminus was at Baghdad (North) on the opposite bank of the Tigris and was connected to the Basra line by a wagon ferry. This line terminated at Kirkuk in the north east of the country.

The standard gauge section was the final portion of the German inspired "Berlin-Bagdad Bahn" started by them before World

41

War I. This had reached Aleppo by the end of the War, and was then pushed on by the Turks and the French up to the Iraq border. The Germans had constructed sixty miles of track at the Baghdad end before the end of World War I, but the final link up was not until 1940. The Taurus Express now ran the whole distance from Hydar Pasha (Istanbul) to Baghdad. The Baghdad terminus was adjacent to the metre gauge's West station.

Neither section possessed much modern equipment, and as the greater part of the track was on sand ballast, speeds were very low. The original equipment of the metre gauge had come from India and Indian practice and signalling prevailed. The locomotive stock consisted almost entirely of "H" Class 4–6–0s; as Iraq had an abundance of oil and a scarcity of water, all engines on both the metre and standard gauge were oil burners and towed a water tank wagon behind the tender to augment the supply. The majority of the stock provided for all classes were bogie vehicles, if not the originals, modelled on those which had been supplied at the end of World War I by various Indian Railways. Most of the upper class carriages, like their Indian counterparts, were non corridor with a separate lavatory for each compartment; no extra charge was made for lying down accomodation, but no bedding was supplied. There were a few rakes of modern stock running in the Baghdad Mail which surpassed anything on the metre gauge in India. This train 1st and 2nd class only was corridored and vestibuled with a restaurant car and a 1st class air conditioned coach. Accomodation was in two berth compartments (lower berths only) in 1st class and four berths in 2nd. A supplement was charged for air conditioned berths with bedding supplied. There was just about sufficient capacity on the metre gauge for Iraq's own needs but little to spare for the British Forces. It was possible to run a daily Mail and Passenger on the Basra line and the equivalent on that to Kirkuk.

By contrast the situation on the standard gauge was catastrophic. The opening of the link to Mosul had come at a time when Iraq, because of the War, was unable to obtain any new locomotive or coaching stock, and what sufficed for a sparse service on sixty miles of track, was quite inadequate for an international link. The locomotive stock consisted of a few 2–6–0s built by Borsig of Berlin in 1914. The coaching stock was mainly four wheeled box like 3rd class, looking like converted goods wagons, which they probably were, and one or two bogie 1st and 2nd composites. These latter had been imported by the British Forces at the end of World War I, and looked very like the older LSWR corridor coaches; they had been converted to provide lying down accomodation and had end doors without any bellows connection.

The Iraq Railways solution was to combine their stock with the twice weekly Taurus Express. This train, although classified by the WL Company as one of their "Luxe" Grand Expresses, would not have been recognised as such in Europe, as it admitted 1st, 2nd and 3rd Class ordinary passengers and was a mixed train over parts of its route. At this time, I travelled on it only as far as Aleppo, although after the War my wife and I did the whole run to Hydar Pasha. The make up at Baghdad was a WL Restaurant Car, a WL Sleeping Car of type "SG" and a WL Fourgon, all for Hyder Pasha with an Iraq Railways 1st and 2nd composite and a number of 3rd class vehicles for Mosul. It left in the evening and arrived at Mosul the following morning – here the Iraq vehicles were replaced by Syrian coaches of the LSB (*Ligne Syrìenne à Baghdad*), a 1st and 2nd composite and 3rd class corridor coaches of European type, together with a long string of goods wagons. The frontier station of Tel Kotchek was reached about midday; this had been the railhead for many years and the WL Company had maintained a Rest House for through passengers going on by motor to Kirkuk. The Iraq engine was replaced here by an identical machine, except that, instead of "IR", it had a Syrian eagle on the cab sides and the letters LSB. The goods wagons were taken off and replaced by a new string which had cleared Syrian Customs. This was done with much blowing of horns in the French fashion, and when all was ready, the train set off for its fifty mile run across a finger of Syrian territory, known as the "Bec de Canard", the "Duck's Bill". After the station of Tel Zouane, the Express entered Turkey and left my jurisdiction; in actual fact Syria came under the British IX Army, but for convenience, Iraq Force was dealing with railway security up to the Turkish frontier.

Iraq and Syria were extremely hot in summer, over 100°F, and all Iraq upper class carriages had large swivel fans of Indian type and the WL sleeping car's compartments had a small fan; by contrast the upper class carriages of the LSB had no such amenity. The type "SG" sleeping cars in use in the Taurus were a modification, for use in Turkey, of the "S" type used in Europe; they were blue all steel cars built in the late twenties, and comprised seven double and three single compartments – originally they had eight doubles, but the modification consisted of converting a double at one end into a washroom for the new end compartment and a pantry for the attendant. The four doubles at the other end did not have separate wash basins within the compartments, but were grouped in pairs with a washroom between and common to each pair. Three singles and two doubles followed, each with its wash basin within the compartment and finally a double with a separate washroom. The Restaurant car and fourgon were standard vehicles and call for no comment.

There was no double line within Iraq, Syria or eastern Turkey; the Iraq Railways used the single line block token apparatus usual in India with fixed signals at all crossing stations, but in Syria the "crossing order" system was in vogue, with no fixed signals – a fixed warning target and a pointsman sitting on the station loop points with a flag or lamp was deemed sufficient. The station buildings in Iraq, with the exception of Mosul, which boasted a Refreshment Room, were little better than those of an Indian wayside station. Baghdad (West) standard gauge was a very odd station – the single platform was not on a line proceeding in the direction of travel, but on one going to the engine shed and sidings. The three WL vehicles and the Iraq Railways upper class coach were drawn up at the platform, but the locomotive followed by a string of 3rd class four wheelers would take up a position on the main line; at departure time the carriages at the platform would be pulled out backwards by a shunting engine and pushed up on to the train proper.

Iraq in the summer of 1941 was occupied by the British Forces, but was not at war with the Axis Powers, although she had broken off diplomatic relations and expelled their nationals; she still had relations with the Vichy French. Syria was occupied by Commonwealth Forces and administered by the Free French. In view of Iraq's sovereignty, I had no responsibility for the physical security of her railways, although I did allot one of my newly raised Field Security Sections to work on them. My journeys on the metre gauge Basra Mail were mundane, but things were different on the international line where I became involved in counter-espionage.

The Taurus Express was one of the only two routes open from Axis Europe to the rest of the World, (the other was via Lisbon) so it was imperative to put on some form of control, not only to deter enemy agents, but also to gain information of conditions inside Europe. This became one of my jobs as Head of the I(b) section of the General Staff in Baghdad, but before I could start, I had to decide on personnel and venue. Nothing could be done inside neutral Iraq, but luckily the frontier station at Tel Kotchek was physically on Syrian soil. Many of my British security personnel were from the Intelligence Corps, which included NCOs of good education and European language qualifications. I withdrew some three or four such from their sections and dispatched them to Tel Kotchek. Their duties were to accompany the Syrian Sureté on their passport inspections, list all through passengers with nationality, passport numbers and any other useful information. They were to note particularily any passengers coming from Axis countries and point them out to an NCO travelling on the train. The latter would contact them, often over a drink in the restaurant car, and if they had anything interesting to recount, would report this on arrival at Baghdad, where they would be visited by a member of the Intelligence Staff. They were warned that they were to deal only with the Intelligence aspect and not to get involved in smuggling, or anything of that kind. My office prepared weekly lists of travellers which were sent to an number of Intelligence agencies – Security Intelligence Middle East (SIME), the Security Intelligence (Ib)

45

sections of HQ Middle East and HQ IX Army, the British Embassy, Baghdad and so on.

The next problem was to get the co-operation of thr WL staff, who belonged to the Turkish Division of the Company. The Headquarters were at Paris and were therefore under the effective control of the Germans; the Company had no office in Baghdad and the reservation of berths and any local provisioning was the responsibility of the well known firm of travel agents, Cooks, who had been a subsidary of the Wagon Lits and, therefore, was under the control of the Custodian of Enemy Property in London. The Turkish employees travelled on a special Company Identity Card which was recognised by Turkey, Syria and Iraq. It was well known that Conductors and sleeping car Attendants were required to observe their passengers and report anything unusual or interesting to the frontier control police and customs. This had the advantage for travellers that, when travelling in a sleeping car, they were seldom disturbed at night; it meant also that any employee that who did not co-operate would be declared persona non grata by the country concerned and would probably lose his job. The staff at first were reluctant to work for us and considered that, as we could not take away their Identity Cards, they had nothing to fear. To persuade them, a regime of rigorous searches was instituted at Tel Kotchek, where having the assistance of the Free French authorities, we could do much as we pleased. The searches took the form of ransacking the linen cupboards, pulling the bedding off the berths, taking the foodstuffs out of the icebox, unscrewing the advertisements and so on, and then leaving the staff to put it all back. Many have asked what effect this had on the running of the train – the short answer is that it made it very late, but this was a small matter as it was often anything up to eight hours late when it arrived from Turkey. I am glad to say that, in a very short time, the Turks decided to co-operate, especially when they learnt that we paid for information.

I made a number of journeys to Tel Zouane, as this was the station for Kamechlié, the principal town in that part of Syria, where I could always get a bed with our Political Liason Officer;

in fact, whenever I felt that a change was needed from routine in Baghdad, I would apply for an official tour "to inspect the Passport Post at Tel Kotchek". This entitled me to a 1st class rail warrant, and I then booked my sleeping car berth at Cooks, for which I had to pay myself. One of the joys of the trip was the French cooking in the restaurant car, a welcome change from the meals served by our Indian servants in the Baghdad Officers' Messes. My most exciting trip was a journey to and from Beirut in the autumn of 1941. I was due for a months leave in India but I thought it would be more fun to go to Beirut by train, and as I had had no real instruction in security work, to study this with the real professionals, the British Field Security Sections in Aleppo and Beirut. I would be able also to visit Headquarters IX Army and discuss the regularisation of our work in the Duck's Bill, so I approached my GSO I, the Head of Intelligence, with a proposition – if he would auhorise an official tour, which meant that my fares would be paid., I would pay my Hotel bills and promise to spend 50% of my time working; to my satisfaction my GSO I agreed to my suggestion.

The Treaty of Sèvres, which ended the War with Turkey, drew the northern frontier of Syria along the line of the Berlin-Bagdad Bahn but with the railway track actually in Turkey. This gave a detached section of the LSB in the Duck's Bill and a detached section of the Turkish National Railways between there and Tchoban Bey, north of Aleppo; additionally the line was physically on the frontier, so the station buildings were in Turkey, but on the other side of the line would be a small Fort flying the "Tricoleur". The Turks and French had an understanding about the transfer of rolling stock, the movement of sealed wagons, and even the transit of troops in uniform from one enclave to the other without any formalities. None of this applied to me so I had to obtain civilian clothes and a Passport describing me as a "British Government servant" to avoid internment as a belligerent.

I bought some civilian clothes and visited the British Consul who issued me with the appropriate Passport; my next visit was to Cooks where I booked my sleeping berth. The journey to Tel

Zouane was without incident, and on the evening of the second day we crossed the Turkish frontier into the station of Nusaybin; here our Syrian engine came off and a real monster came on – a German built Turkish 2–10–0. The goods wagons were taken away and a Turkish bogie mail van put on and we were away – an Express at last. This did not last as I noticed that when we arrived at Aleppo, the tail of goods wagons had re-appeared. I stayed several days in Aleppo and then set off to Beirut.

The railway southwards from Aleppo was the DHP (*Damas, Hama et Prolongements*); it had both standard and narrow gauge components. The former ran due south from Aleppo through Hama and Homs to Rayak, close to Baalbek, on the narrow gauge Beirut-Damascus line. A branch from Homs ran through the mountains to terminate at Tripoli, whence a connecting bus took passengers to Beirut. In the following year, the Royal Engineers built a new line down the coast through Beirut to join the Palestine Railways at Acre; the formation of the State of Israel meant the cessation of services on the southern portion, but a daily railcar from Aleppo to Beirut was still shown in Cook's Time Table for 1973. The narrow gauge lines were based on Damascus and were built to the curious gauge of 1.05 metres (3ft 3¼in), found elsewhere only on minor lines in Algeria. They comprised the Beirut line with rack sections over the Lebanese mountains, the Hedjaz Railway south to Jordan via Deraa, and a line from Deraa through Galilee to Haifa. The DHP had considerably more trains than the very sparse service on the LSB, at least a train a day on all lines – the Beirut and Homs lines had two. The most important was the Tripoli service, which had a day time railcar carrying all three classes and night mixed train, which also conveyed a sleeping car. The latter was part of the Taurus on two days a week as the "SG" car continued to Hydar Pasha, but on other days an old teak car was provided, probably a survivor of five such cars sent to Asiatic Turkey in 1924.

I travelled outwards by the railcar, but returned by night in the sleeping car changing into the Taurus at Aleppo. There was an enlivening incident on the day after we had left Aleppo – we were travelling along the section where the railway was also the

48

frontier, when there was an almighty crash, followed by another, and two windows in the corridor on the Syrian side were smashed. I naturally concluded that someone had shot at us. but no, it was the Bedouin using the train for target practice for their slings – shades of David and Goliath!. Later the WL Conductor came to my compartment and said in French – "Mon Capitaine, I see from your Passport that you are Monsieur Mains, a British Government servant, but I know that you are Monsieur le Capitaine Mains, the British Army Controller of Passports – Mon Capitaine, when we arrive at Tel Zouane, your Sergeant will come on board to examine the Passports, please tell him to report this incident to the French Officier du Service Spéciale at Kamechlié and ask him to send out his Circassians to beat up those Bedouin". This I duly did.

Shortly after my return to Baghdad, there was the problem of the repatriation of Axis nationals from Afghanistan and Persia; these countries had agreed to expel them if we would arrange their return home. The only practicable route was rail and ship to Basra for one party and road to Baghdad for the other; the remainder of the route, of course, was by rail to Hydar Pasha. The difficulty was the provision of rolling stock, and this was aggravated by the order that they must travel in "soft" class, and not on hard seated 3rd class; neither could they travel in non corridor coaches as this would make their guarding very difficult. The metre gauge could provide sufficient corridor stock, but only by cutting the the carriages on the Baghdad-Basra Mail by about one third; causing much grumbling by prospective travellers. The stock position on the standard gauge had improved, as at the time of the invasion of southern Persia, some standard gauge coaches en route from Germany, were in the Baghdad railway workshops having metre gauge bogies fitted for their transit to Basra; they had been requisitioned and handed over to the Iraq Railways. Even so there was insufficient stock to provide two trains right through to Hydar Pasha. The problem was solved by Cooks hiring two trains of upper class stock, each with a WL Restaurant Car, from the Turkish Railways.

A further difficulty arose over Security – the possibility of a

German advance through the Caucasus on to the Iraq oilfields, had led to a large build up of troops and stores. Most of the dumps and depots were located close to the railway line at Basra, Baghdad and Mosul. and it was most undesirable that any Axis nationals should see them. I proposed, therefore, that the party should come ashore and entrain at Basra at night; their train would then lie up at a wayside station in the desert during the day, tranship at Baghdad at night, lie up again during the following day and go through Mosul in the dark. This plan brought the wrath of the administrative and transportation staffs down on my head. I was told that the plan was unnecessary and absurd – that it would cause administrative difficulties and increase the hire charges of the Turkish train and so on. The matter went to the General and to our great relief he came down on our side.

Shortly after this I was promoted Major on upgrading to a second grade General Staff Officer (GSO II) and ordered to return to India to take up a new appointment in the East.

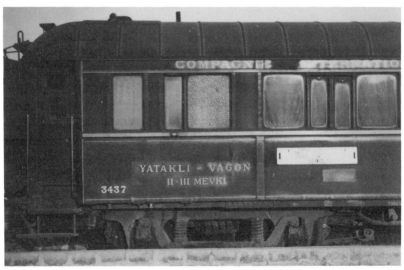

Taurus Express Sleeping Car 'SG' type.   *John Price*

Turkish Railways 2-10-0 locomotive.

John Price

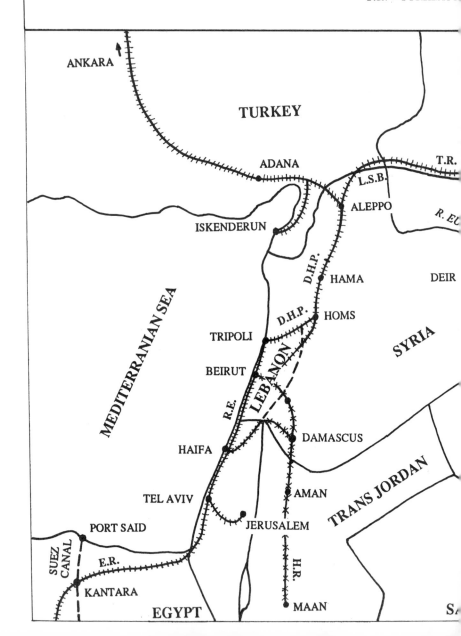

THE M[...]

Sh[...]

RAILWAYS GAUGE
STANDARD 4' 8 ¾"
METRE 3' 3"
OTHER 3' 5 ¼"

E.R.—EGYPTIAN [...]
P.R.—PALESTINE [...]
R.E.—ROYAL EN[...]
T.R.—TURKISH R[...]

ANKARA

TURKEY

ADANA

ISKENDERUN

MEDITERRANEAN SEA

T.R.

L.S.B.

ALEPPO

R. EU[...]

D.H.P.

HAMA

DEIR

D.H.P.

HOMS

TRIPOLI

BEIRUT

LEBANON

SYRIA

R.E.

HAIFA

DAMASCUS

TEL AVIV

AMAN

TRANS JORDAN

PORT SAID

JERUSALEM

SUEZ CANAL

E.R.

H.R.

KANTARA

EGYPT

MAAN

SA[...]

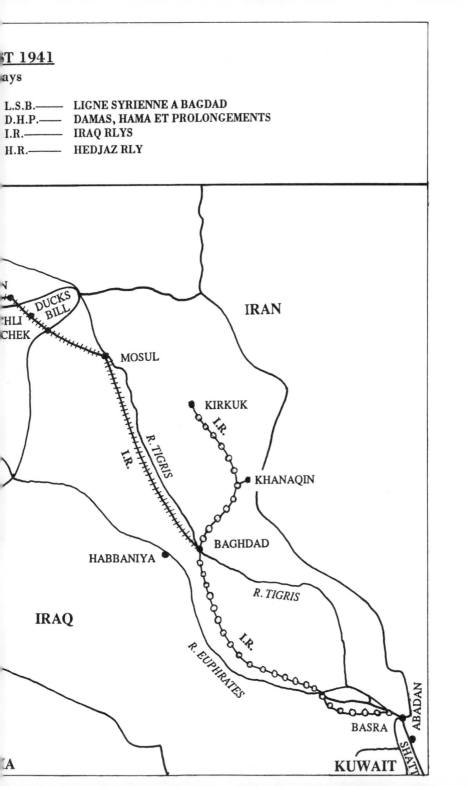

L.S.B.——— LIGNE SYRIENNE A BAGDAD
D.H.P.——— DAMAS, HAMA ET PROLONGEMENTS
I.R.——— IRAQ RLYS
H.R.——— HEDJAZ RLY

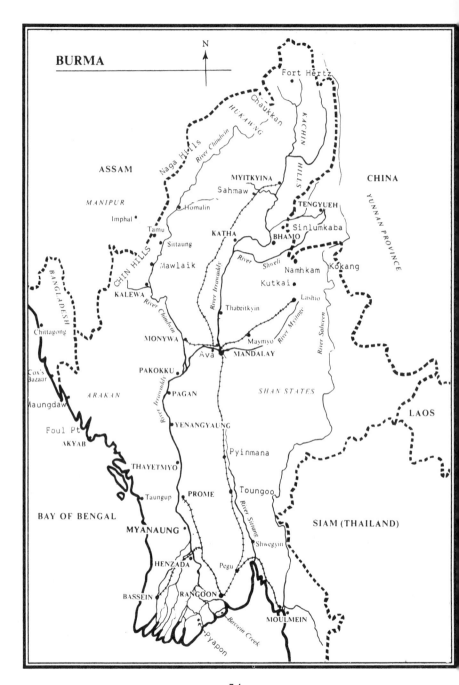

BURMA

N

ASSAM

CHINA

MANIPUR

Fort Hertz

Chaukkan

HUKAWNG

Naga Hills

River Chindwin

KACHIN HILLS

YUNNAN PROVINCE

MYITKYINA

Sahmaw

Imphal

Homalin

Tamu

KATHA

TENGYUEH

Sinlumkaba

BHAMO

Sittaung

CHIN HILLS

Mawlaik

River Shweli

Namhkam

Kokang

Kutkai

BANGLADESH

KALEWA

River Chindwin

River Irrawaddy

Thabeitkyin

Lashio

Chittagong

MONYWA

Maymyo

River Myitnge

River Salween

Ava

MANDALAY

Cox's Bazaar

PAKOKKU

ARAKAN

PAGAN

SHAN STATES

LAOS

Maungdaw

River Irrawaddy

YENANGYAUNG

Foul Pt

AKYAB

Pyinmana

THAYETMYO

Taungup

PROME

Toungoo

River Sittang

BAY OF BENGAL

SIAM (THAILAND)

MYANAUNG

Shwegyin

HENZADA

Pegu

BASSEIN

RANGOON

Bassein Creek

Pyapon

MOULMEIN

54

CHAPTER V

RETREAT FROM BURMA – 1942

I managed, with some difficulty, to get a flight from Basra to Karachi, and then went on to Delhi by the Karachi and Frontier Mails, changing at Lahore. My destination was to be Rangoon and I had been appointed to head the security section in Headquarters Burma Army; My new Chief was Lieutenant Colonel Philip Gwyn. Although a Japanese invasion of Burma was imminent, and, presumably our presence in Rangoon was urgently required, Army Headquarters, India, had great difficulty in getting us there – so much so that I was given a week's leave, which was spent in Dehra Dun. On my return I was told that Philip Gwyn and I were to be flown from Calcutta to Rangoon in a DC 2 (the forerunner of the famous DC 3 or "Dakota") of the Indian Air Force, but the problem was to find us an air passage to Calcutta. I was hoping that this would prove to be impossible and that we should have to go by train, as up to now I had not travelled on the Delhi to Calcutta Mail. Unfortunately, a place was found for us on the Tata Air Lines daily flight and after a night's stop over in Calcutta, we duly landed at Mingaladon Airport at Rangoon on 20th of January 1941 in the middle of an air raid.

I was only in Burma from then until I arrived back in India in mid May, so I had little time to observe the Burma Railways. However, on several occasions I became involved in assisting them in various ways, notably during the evacuation of Rangoon and, received as a result of a report by the Chief Commissioner of Railways to General Alexander, the Army Commander, the award of a "Mention in Dispatches".

Prior to the separation of Burma from India in 1937, the State owned and operated Burma Railways came under the Railway Board in Delhi, but because of distance and absence of any physical connection, the Burma railways had been allowed to be semi independent in matters of locomotives and rolling stock.

The system, of 2000 route miles, was of metre gauge and single line, with the exception of a long double section from Rangoon to above Toungoo on the main Mandalay line, and in the vicinity of Rangoon itself. The main line had two important branches – one from Pegu to Martaban, the ferry terminal for Moulmein; this crossed the Sittang River by the famous (or infamous) bridge, which was blown with a large number of British units still on the wrong side, and the other penetrated into the southern Shan States. From Mandalay, after a reversal, the main line continued to Myitkyina in the far north of the country crossing the Irrawady by the long Ava Bridge. A branch went east to Lashio in the northern Shan States, which was the railhead for for the "China Road". There was a secondary main line to from Rangoon to Prome on the Irrawady, where it connected with the river steamers to Mandalay and the north. Other minor branches do not affect this account. The majority of the lines were on the flat plain, without any tunnels or steep gradients; the exceptions were the two branches into the Shan States; both of which climbed into the hills with gradients steep enough to require reversing stations, and to work these lines the Burma Railways had acquired both "Garrett" and "Mallet" locomotives.

My duties in Burma should have been much the same as they had been in Iraq, that is to organise Security Intelligence and to that end to raise Field Security sections, but the difference was that Burma was engaged in a war from the day that I arrived and as a result, I found myself and such security personnel, as it had been possible collect, doing all sorts of odd jobs, most of which were of a civil or military police nature. This was because there were no British Military Police in the country and the Corps of Indian Military Police was only just being raised. As soon as the Japanese invasion started the Civil Police just melted away. Many of this Force were not Burmese but Indians; the Rangoon City Police was mainly Punjabi Moslems and Sikhs, and they were in mortal terror of the Japanese. Confusion has occurred over the existence of the "Burma Military Police"; this was a civil para military force recruited mainly from Indians and Gurkhas to act as armed police in the Districts for anti dacoit (bandit) work, Treasury guards and so on.

56

I had only one month of relative peace in which to try to organise security in general and raising security sections in particular, as on the 20th of February, the Army Commander, General Hutton, ordered the activation of the "E" plan, which was the preliminary evacuation of Rangoon. By this time, the Intelligence School at Karachi had sent me a GSO III, Bill Talbot, as my No 2, and a number of Field Security Officers designate; I also had a Field Security section of sorts, consisting of a British Officer, some five or six British volunteers mainly from the Gloucesters, Rangoon's garrison battalion, and a Jemadar and six Indian ranks ex Karachi. I decided to retain this section in Rangoon for the time being, and to send Bill Talbot and the remainder up to rear Headquarters at Maymyo to raise and train new sections. One of our difficulties was the equipment of this section as everything was in short supply, and units were loathe to let any man take his equipment or arms with him; We managed, however, to obtain a number of police "riot guns", pump handle shot guns, and lathis, which were going to be of infinately more use in the days ahead than conventional arms. It was fortunate too, that the F.S.O, of this makeshift section, Captain McGilp of the 5th Gurkhas and a peacetime field worker with the Anglo Iranian Oil Company, was both energetic and dependable.

No sooner had the evacuation started, than I was ordered to take McGilp's section to Rangoon station and place myself at the disposal of the railway authorities. The senior Railway Officer in the Rangoon area was Lieutenant Colonel Brewitt, who when the Railway had been militarised, had been given this rank and appointed Deputy Director of the Burma Railways and it was to him that I reported. All the subordinate staff had decamped by this time, and what was left consisted of a handful of Officers, mostly British, but including a young Burmese Assistant Traffic Superintendent, a few Anglo Burmese traffic staff and guards and a fair number of Anglo Burmese drivers and firemen. The main staff problem was the complete absence of Indian coal coolies and this resulted in the already overworked engine crews having to coal their own engines. Our task was to oversee the general security of the area, to ensure that the trains were loaded in an orderly manner and to prevent riot, and finally, the most important, to protect the railway staff from interference or attack. This was a task which should have been carried out by the Rangoon City Police, but by this time this Force had shrunk from its normal strength of about two thousand to less than sixty, as the Indian constables were awaiting evacuation and all that was left was five senior Officers and about forty five Anglo Burmese Sergeants. McGilp had obtained a requisitioned house near the Station and I moved in with him, but took my meals with the Railway Officers who had very kindly asked me to join their Mess.

The railway plan for the evacuation was to run one through train daily to Mandalay, for the so called "Priveliged Evacuees", those who had been guaranteed a safe passage out of Rangoon, and a shuttle service to Prome for the rest. This shuttle service gave little trouble, other than the shortage of staff, as the line was going away from the front line and was reasonably secure from enemy attention. Our main concern was to keep order, prevent dangerous overcrowding, and to see that the trains were filled with people and not with baggage; a strict rule of one package per person had to be enforced. Many tried to move their entire household or stock in trade, and heart rending appeals were made to us that their abandonement would mean financial ruin. Had we been dishonest, we could have made our fortunes for bribes were freely offered.

The "privileged evacuees" train was a real headeache as it ran straight through to Mandalay. and every one wanted to get on board, whether they had any right to or not. The evacuees were a very mixed bunch, extending through every stratum of society from Government subordinate and clerical staff to hospital sweepers and menials, the latter classes prone to panic and without discipline. The actual running of this train posed problems also, as the main line ran via Pegu and, after the Sittang disaster was close to the front line with the distinct possibility that the Japanese might infiltrate our forces and cut the line. There were no staff in any station between Rangoon and Pegu, rendering the normal block system inoperative, nor was the track patrolled by the usual permanent way gangs. Luckily the line was double so the possibility of collision was small. Rangoon to Pegu was made one long block section and, when telephone advice of the arrival of a train was received at Rangoon, another was launched "into the blue", with no knowledge of how it was faring until it arrived at Pegu. It must be emphasised that the evacuee special was not the only train running on this section; supply trains had to be run for the 17th Indian Division at Pegu, and further trains provided to move the newly arrived 63rd Indian Brigade up to Pegu.

Colonel Brewitt asked me to take over the loading of the Mandalay train, merely giving me a list of the Departments entitled to travel on each day with a rough estimate of their numbers. The train was due to depart about 3 pm, but by noon the station was a seething mass of humanity and baggage; there was no public address system so we had to do the best we could with a megaphone. The first essential was to call inside the station the senior official of each party and to check with him the exact number of travellers. He was then told to return to his party and explain that they were were to behave quietly and not to panic, as places would be found for all. The official concerned was further ordered to report back with a reliable man who would act as a guide.

As soon as the train drew up at the platform, I, personally, allotted the accomodation, marking the compartment doors in chalk with the name of the party. The leaders and guides were then brought to the gate and the leader of the first party to load, stood by the entrance gate through which his party had to pass in single file; he was supported by two Field Security men with lathis at the ready. The respective leaders had been told that they must identify personally each member of their party as they passed in. The gate was then opened and each party was led in turn to their accomodation. Any one trying to gatecrash or with excess baggage was given a whack from a lathi and pushed back from the gate; the legitimate traveller was later allowed in after divesting

59

himself of his surplus baggage. On the whole, except for the noise, which was greatly in excess of the hubbub normally to be heard in a busy eastern station, the loading was orderly enough, although every now and then there were disputes or even fights which had to be quelled. I recall one incident of a man so panic-stricken that he had lost all sense of reason and was even trampling on other people in his anxiety to get into the train. He was completely deaf to any appeals and as panic is infectious, I hit him smartly on the head with my lathi; he collapsed, but before we had time to attend to him, he got up and proceeded quietly, if shakily, to the train.

On the second day a nasty and what might well have been a very serious incident occurred. I was allotting accomodation, when I was told that a body of well over one hundred Indian Constables of the City Police, in uniform, were congregated in the station forecourt demanding passage to Mandalay. They were to be evacuated to Prome, where it was hoped to reform them for service in other Districts, but Colonel Brewitt had not been informed of this. It was unfortunate that a story, partly true, was current that on the capture of Tavoy, the Japanese had handed over any Police who had remained at their posts to the mob, and this accounted for the panic. They were threatening to storm the barrier, and, as appeals for calm were of no avail, all that could be done was to draw up my four or five men and warn the Police that should they attempt this, they would be fired on. This threat had little effect, but the situation was saved by the arrival of the Deputy Commissioner of Police, Mr Bestall, who had come to make arrangements for their transport to Prome. He grabbed the megaphone and managed to calm them. He then told them that he was thoroughly ashamed of them; they had been guaranteed a passage to Prome and that would be honoured. In the meantime they would be under my orders and anyone who disobeyed would not be put on the train and stood a good chance of being shot.

After the departure of the Mandalay train, we set about loading the Police into a train for Prome. They were orderly enough, but it transpired that on their way to the station they had systematically looted the cloth market. Every man had at least one bundle of brand new bolts of cloth, sheets, towels, and so on, as well as his personal kit. In the altercations which followed, some of my Field Security, particularily the Indian ranks, gave any policeman slow to relinquish his loot a beating with their lathis. In the middle of this fracas, the Commissioner, Mr Prescott, arrived in a furious rage and demanded to know why the Field Security were beating the Police. I replied hotly, regardless of his high rank, that I should like to know why he had sent the Police to the station without prior warning, why had they become a disorderly mob and why had they looted the cloth market. I then added, for good measure, that he should be thankful that I had not opened fire on them. This incident caused a coolness between us, which was aggravated when a day or so later, I was appointed Assistant Military Governor of Rangoon in charge of Law and Order.

Before concluding the saga of the railway evacuation, I would like to put on record that the highest praise should go to to the railwaymen who remained at duty and, in particular, to the Anglo Burmese drivers and firemen. It takes great courage to take out a train towards the enemy lines without an escort, but even greater courage to bring it back for another load, once you have reached comparative safety. The work of the fighter pilots of the RAF and AVG (American Volunteer Group), part of the Chinese Army) also deserves great praise. We were spared air raids, which would have made our task quite impossible, thanks to their seeing off the Japanese before they could attain their targets.

After about five days the situation at the station had become quiet enough at the station to leave matters in the hands of McGilp and his section. I had hoped to set off for Maymyo, but, as it so happened, I was sent back into the City to take charge of Law and Order until the bitter end, but that is recorded elsewhere. The District Locomotive Superintendent, Rangoon, retired near me and up to his death, a few years ago, we argued whether his last train went under the bridge at the western end of Rangoon station before or after my small Field Security party went over it.

I eventually arrived at Maymyo after evading capture at the

61

action at Taukkyan Bend, and a period of relative calm set in, during which three Field Security sections were raised. I decided to utilise this period to familiarise myself with the country and its special security problems. Trips to Lashio and Mandalay were made by road, but I persauded Colonel Brewitt to lend me a Railway Officer's saloon for a third trip. This was to be to Shewbo and Monywa in central Burma. Shewbo, on the Myitkyina line, was a small cantonment, which had been taken over by the 2nd Echelon of Burma Army – the section which deals with the documentation of officers and soldiers on active sevice. It employed a vast number of Indian and Burmese clerks, many of them civilians who had their families with them. It was evident that the evacuation of this multitude would be a great problem if and when the time came. There was also an airfield in constant use bringing in reinforcements from India and taking out wounded and such European women and children as had still not left the country. Monwya, a river port on the Chindwin, would become important if the Burma Army had to retreat on India by the overland route.

Officers' saloons were rare in the British Isles as railway officers would normally return home each night or, if they could not, would easily find accomodation. The great distances and the paucity of hotels or similar accomodation in the East caused the railway administrations to provide a large stock of saloons. They varied from the palatial vehicles of the senior officers to the four wheelers of the junior staff. Even these were extremely comfortable – at one end was the main saloon, containing two sofa berths, a table, chairs and cupboards, rather like the interior of a modern caravan. A corridor led out of this past the bathroom, with its basin, shower and lavatory to the servant's quarters, comprising a kitchen, living space and an Indian type latrine. The saloon could be detached at any station with a siding and re-attached to any other train as required. I had hoped that my saloon would have been sent up to Maymyo so that I could see this severely graded section with its reversing stations, but Colonel Brewitt, for operating reasons, asked me to join it at Mandalay.

I duly motored down with my Madrassi servant, and plenty of food and drink, and found the saloon, a small bogie vehicle, attached to the rear of the daily train to Myitkyina. Mandalay is shown on most small scale maps as the junction for the Lashio and Myitkyina branches, but, in fact, the actual junction is at Myohaung, one station to the south. This station had only two full length running loops so no trains terminated there but proceeded onward to Mandalay Yard. We ran through Myohaung and taking the right hand road were soon rumblimg over the great Ava Bridge and into Ywataung station. This was not only the junction for the Monywa line but the Headquarters of an administrative District of the Burma Railways and contained the offices and residences of the District Traffic and Locomotive Superintendents and other officers and staff. We had left Mandalay in mid morning and arrived at Shwebo in early afternoon; my saloon was cut off and parked in a siding, while I went and made my number with the local civil and military authorities. I arranged with the Station Master to have the saloon attached to the Mandalay train which was coming through during the night. I decided to carry on through to Mandalay rather than await the Monywa train at Ywataung; had I known what awaited me at Mandalay, I might well have made a different decision.

I awoke in Mandalay yard and after breakfast arranged for the saloon to be attached to the Monywa train. Mandalay station ran north and south with the principal platform adjacent to the station buildings and offices. There were four platforms in all, and parallel to them on the far side was the marshalling yard, full to overflowing with wagons, laden with every type of military store, which had been evacuated from the south. The railway administration was still trying to sort them out and work them away to the various depots to which they had originally been consigned. Unfortunately, in the confusion and haste in which they had been dispatched, few had been properly labelled and their contents were largely unknown.

The starting signal was off at about 11 am and I was sitting quietly awaiting the departure, when there was the most tremendous explosion. My first impression was that the engine

63

had blown up, but then there was a second explosion followed by a third, and I now realised that an air raid was in progress – my instinctive reaction was to dive under the berth. On reflection some time later, I realised that the wooden body of the saloon would not have resisted bomb splinters, and that the floor level of a metre gauge coach was just right to receive the maximum amount of blast from a bomb bursting nearby. As soon as the explosions ceased, I emerged from the saloon; it was quite impossible to see anything as the dust raised by the bombing was worse than a desert sand storm. This was just beginning to settle when down came another stick of bombs, which sent me racing to the Station Master's office, which was protected by baffle walls. In my haste I slipped on the broken glass, which littered the platform from the shattered roof, and came down cutting a nasty gash in my hand. As soon as the dust had settled again, and those of us who were on the station had recovered our wits, we took stock of the damage.

This, fortunately, was comparatively light as the Japanese were using high fragmentation anti-personnel bombs to terrorise the civilian population. The first bombs had landed ahead of the engine of my train and continued diagonally from south east to north west across the yard, so by the time they came level with my saloon there were several lines of steel goods wagons for protection. The craters were small and the damage done to the track was minimal and could be put right in a short time. Mercifully the bombs had not fallen on the actual station or its approaches or the loss of life would have been very heavy. There had been no warning whatsoever and the platform and forecourt had been crammed with passengers, food sellers and beggars – all the turbid conglomeration of a normal station in the East. The main danger seemed to be from one or two small fires in the marshalling yard.

There was a shunting engine in steam, with a driver at the north end of the yard, but the signalman, not unnaturally but very unfortunately, had decamped. The north signal box, although small, was fully interlocked so the points and signals remained locked unless the levers were pulled in the correct sequence.

Colonel Brewitt and other railway officers arrived on the scene but no one had any knowledge of the interlocking – so – the projected use of the shunting engine to pull wagons away from the fires had to be abandoned in favour of manpower – we pushed the wagons. After a fairly lengthy session of pushing, my hand became extremely painful and was bleeding quite freely; Brewitt suggested that it was time to let the Railway Doctor have a look at it. There was a railway dispensary in a bungalow immediately in front of the station forecourt, and I went to it. The doctor put in the necessary stitches, bandaged up my hand and suggested that I went to the Railway Officer's Mess next door to get a drink.

I was just approaching the Mess, when I happened to notice a slit trench and simultaneously there was another tremendous explosion. Now, whether I jumped into the trench or was blown in by the blast, I shall never know, but as I went in, I noticed that the whole front of the Mess was bulging out and collapsing. After a while, when all seemed quiet again, I got out and saw that the station had become a total wreck; the buildings were a shambles, the overbridge had come down, and badly damaged coaches and wagons were lying about in heaps like so many broken toys. It was later ascertained that the damage was caused by a wagon loads of RAF bombs, exploding in the fire; the presence of which no one had any knowledge.

This incident put paid to any idea of going to Monywa by train, in fact, Mandalay station was never used again; all trains terminated at Myohaung and the administration moved over to the District Offices at Ywataung. There was nothing I could do in Mandalay as the city itself, had been almost totally destroyed, so I returned to Maymyo by road. I was lucky to find my Madrassi servant, Manoel, quite unhurt; his comment on the incident was – "too much bombing, Sah, too much bombing". He made up for whatever he had suffered by drinking the better part of a bottle of my gin on the way up to Maymyo.

It was not long after this that the Generalissimo, Chiang Kai-Shek, visited Maymyo to confer with the Army and Corps Commanders, Generals Alexander and Slim. Burma Railways laid on a train of luxurious saloon carriages to take him back to

Lashio, and I was required to search it in case any bombs had been planted on it. I also detailed a Field Security party to travel on the train but this was more to safeguard the train crew from the General's escort of Chinese Gendarmerie, than to protect the great man.

Our time in Maymyo came to its inevitable end as we were forced back towards India. Army Headquarters moved to Shwebo and the Chinese took over Maymyo; the situation on the railways was chaotic in the extreme, as on the hill section up to Maymyo, the block system had ceased to exist owing to the staff decamping and the instruments being smashed. This line was carrying a two way traffic – British troop trains coming down and Chinese going up. The Chinese were very indisciplined and their commanders would not believe that two trains could not go in opposite directions on the same line wihout disaster. I had personal experience of this, as, on my way to Shwebo by car, I called in at Ywataung to see if there was anyway I could help Colonel Brewitt and his men. He asked me to take a party of Field Security NCOs to Myohaung, where a bombing raid had caused difficulties and the presence of a Chinese troop train was not helping matters.

The bombing had taken place earlier in the day and, although the station and tracks were undamaged, the signal box had received a near miss and this had jammed the point rodding making it impossible to move the points or the levers. The only way the points could be moved was to unbolt them from the rods, move them over by hand and re-bolt, and this was the job that the railway officers wished the Field Security NCOs to do. The Chinese troop train was standing in one of the three roads waiting to proceed in due course to Lashio. The Chinese, themselves, were in a thoroughly truculent mood, refusing to allow their engine to be moved or to co-operate in any way. The whole countryside was an inferno, every building in sight was ablaze and fusillades of shots rang out from time to time. This was the work of the Chinese soldiers, who had left their train and were amusing themselves by shooting and burning any Burmese that they could find.

We had to push through a crowd of Chinese soldiers to get to the Station Office and ascertain the situation. It appeared that the Chinese train could not leave until a British ammunition train from Maymyo to Shwebo had arrived, and it was essential to get this away and over the Ava Bridge during the hours of darkness. This train on arrival had to await the daily train from Myitkyina before it could leave. The block telegraph was not working so we had no exact knowledge of the whereabouts of these trains or when they were likely to arrive. To make matters worse, only two of the running roads were long enough to accomodate the expected trains, and the Chinese were refusing to allow the engine of their train to be uncoupled so that it could proceed to the next station to get water. They were even threatening to shoot the driver if it was moved without their permission.

We engaged in a lengthy argument with the Chinese General, but meanwhile the Field Security were able to alter the points so that the ammunition train could run into the other long road. Our attempts to explain matters were fruitless as the Chinese repeated parrot fashion – "Chinese Army fighting war, British Army not fighting war, Chinese go first". Meanwhile the ammunition train had arrived, and it had not been in long, before the Myitkyina train was heard whistling at the home signal on the other line. As if the situation was not bad enough, the crew of the ammunition train told us that another supply train was following them down from Maymyo and it would be unsafe to let the Chinese away before it arrived.

We were now faced with a real railway puzzle, and one which would have been difficult enough to solve in normal circumstances. Two single lines, each with a train on it, facing a station of two lines, each blocked by a train. Add to this, darkness, bomb damage, lack of staff, no block telegraph, and last, but by no means least, your Allies threatening to shoot you, and you have a nightmare bad enough to daunt the bravest. However a miracle, in the guise of a senior British Officer of the Liason Mission to the Chinese Army, brought us relief. He accomplished this by haranguing the General with great fluency in his own language and, in a short time, reduced him to order.

Brewitt, meanwhile, had decided that the ammunition train must be got away at all costs; he instructed the train crew to back it up the Myitkyina line as far as the home signal, there to couple on to the incoming train, and thereafter the combined trains were to back away over the Ava Bridge to Ywataung, where they could be sorted out. Matters improved from here on; the second train from Maymyo came in and this allowed the Chinese to be sent on their way to Lashio, while we, in our turn, could return to Ywataung to sleep for what remained of the night. This was the end of my association with the Burma Railways.

Not long after this incident the Ava Bridge was blown severing the connection between the two portions of the railway still operating. The British forces no longer made any use of rail transport, using their own lorries, but the Chinese continued to do so as they had practically no transport of their own. However, even their use of rail transport came to an end very soon afterwards, as the Chinese Commanders continued to insist on running trains when it was unsafe, and as it was impossible to repair the damage caused by the inevitable accidents, movement came to a halt. The Chinese had even arrested Colonel Brewitt on charges of non co-operation, and plans were made to rescue him, using some of my Field Security personnel, but luckily the Chinese relented and released him.

Army Headquarters straggled back into India after a number of vicissitudes and shortly after our arrival in Manipur State, a few of the Intelligence Staff, including Philip Gwyn and myself, were ordered to take ten days "refitting leave" and report back to Headquarters 4 Corps in Assam. We were to take with us as far as Calcutta two "Type X" enciphering machines and two boxes of Cipher books, which we had brought out with us. This was a source of satisfaction as these machines speeded up signal traffic enormously and were in very short supply in the East; on the other hand they had to be manhandled and guarded by us during the journey.

I decided to take my leave in Dehra Dun; our party was moved by lorry to Manipur Road Station where we were issued with 1st Class Railway Warrants to our destinations, although, as it happened, this was not the accomodation in which we travelled, at least for the first part of our journey. The railways in Assam were all of metre gauge with a low carrying capacity and primative signalling and, as a result of the military activity now occurring, had become completely disorganised. No timetable was being adhered to, so we were advised to catch the first train going and travel in whatever accomodation we could find. The train standing in the station when we arrived was the all stations Passenger, and the only accomodation, which was not full to overflowing, was a four wheeled parcel van; which we comandeered. The van had plenty of room for our party including the Type X machines, and we could lie at full length on the shelves provided. At the last minute we allowed on board an American War Correspondent, Alfred Wagg, and it was lucky that we did, as he had a large stock of provisions, without which we would have had a very hungry journey.

The Passenger moved off in mid morning, and we had not gone the ten miles to the next station, before we were delayed for three hours on account of a derailment ahead; after this we proceeded by fits and starts and did not reach Lumding Junction, the first station with a Refreshment Room until after midnight. We finally arrived at Gauhati, the station immediately before the ferry over the Brahmaputra, about 5 pm on the second day, having taken eighteen hours to cover 162 miles. Here we ran into trouble – the authorities wished to side track us to send on the Mail which was not far behind, so that it could connect with the Eastern Bengal Railway's Mail on the other side of the ferry. The line on our side was part of the Assam Bengal Railway's system, and their colleagues on the far bank had long since given up waiting for normal conections; in fact the A.B. Railway's Mail was not really on time but was was actually 24 hours late. We protested strongly, as, if we were held back, we would have had a delay of 24 hours before we could get another train onward. After a furious argument the authorities relented and sent us on.

We dined on the Ferry and, on the other side, were able to obtain one first class berth for Philip Gwyn as he was the senior, and a fair size intermediate class compartment for the rest of us.

The second morning found us at Parbatipur Junction, where we changed into the broad gauge Assam Mail. This was quite a show train as it was one of the three corridor and vestibuled trains then running. "Waggie", as he had become known, told us to take our time transhipping as he would get our seats. When we entered the Restaurant Car, there he was presiding over the breakfast table with an opened bottle of beer at each place. Calcutta was reached at tea time without any further incidents. The whole journey had taken 54 hours instead of the normal 18.

The next day I proceeded onward to Delhi by the East Indian's Toofan (Whirlwind) Express. My journey was normal as far as Cawnpore, some six hours from Delhi, where I was seized with stomache pains so severe that I was unable to detrain when we arrived at Delhi, and had to ask an Officer travelling in my compartment to arrange for an ambulance. As this had to come several miles from the British Military Hospital in Delhi Cantonment, there was a considerable hiatus. A ticket collector arrived and had some difficulty in understanding my predicament – he kept repeating parrot fashion "it is against rule and regulation of Railway for passengers to remain in train when it is going to the siding"; after a while it dawned on him that I was unwell so with an "ooh – you are ill" he left me and the train was shunted away. After what appeared an age two British orderlies appeared with a stretcher and carted me off to hospital. My personal retreat from Burma was over.

Fresh troops arrive at Dinapur Station, Assam, and relieve General Alexander's Burma Army. *Alfred Wagg*

Japanese bombs burst on Mandalay, Good Friday, 1942.

Alfred Wagg

CHAPTER VI

CHAOS, SABOTAGE AND CORRUPTION ON THE ASSAM RAILWAYS – 1942–44.

My stay in Hospital lasted less than a week, but the doctors wished to put me before a Medical Board to assess what convalescent leave I should be granted; this would have automatically cancelled my 4 Corps posting. They agreed, however, that if Army Headquarters would hold my appointment open until the end of one month's ordinary leave, they would merely discharge me. This was done and I spent my leave partly in Dehra Dun and partly in the adjacent hill station of Mussoorie. During my leave Philip Gwyn informed me that he was to be, as a GSO I, the Chief Intelligence Officer of an augmented 4 Corps Headquarters. This Headquarters, newly arrived from England, had been sent up to Assam to command the very meagre military resources facing the Japanese – the 23rd Indian Division of two Brigades only and the 17th Indian Division, refitting after the Burma Retreat. The Corps Headquarters was also to control the Lines of Communication within the Province of Assam, although an *ad hoc* Headquarters, HQ Assam L of C, had been formed in Gauhati to deal with routine matters. The original Intelligence Staff which had come from England consisted of a GSO II, a GSO III for Security and two Intelligence Officers, adequate enough for two Divisions, but not to control the rear administrative areas in addition; hence the augmentation.

The Corps HQ was located at Jorhat in the northern part of the Assam or Brahmaputra valley, where, although somewhat far back it, could command the forward troops. It was not so well placed to deal with the HQ Assam L of C nor the civil Government of the Province, which was located in the hill station of Shillong. The solution was to split the Intelligence staff and locate a strong security section at Gauhati to deal with the L of C. This was to be known as the "Gauhati Intelligence Detachment" with myself as Head although I would retain my position as a GSO II of 4 Corps. We were intended to carry out security work on behalf of the Assam L of C HQ, who had no staff of their own. This ad hoc arrangement continued until the spring of 1943, when 4 Corps relinquished control of the L of C and moved forward to Imphal, the capital of Manipur State. Assam L of C HQ was replaced by HQ 202 L of C Area directly under Eastern Army. I became the Chief Intelligence Officer and the remainder of the Intelligence Detachment became the I(b) section of the Staff. The Area was subdivided into 251 L of C Sub Area at Shillong, No 252 at Dibrugarh and No 253 at Manipur Road Base, each with an Intelligence Officer of their own.

At the end of my leave I left by train for Assam. The journey to Calcutta (Howrah) was by No 10 Doon Express, a semi fast train which is still running today with the same number and roughly the same timings. It joined the East Indian's northern main line at Lakhsar Junction and continued to Lucknow; where it left the newer main line and ran via the older Fyzabad loop to Mughal Serai. The final part of the journey was by the East Indian's "Grand Chord". It left Dehra Dun at about 8 pm and reached Howrah at 7 am on the third day. There was no Restaurant car so breakfast was taken at Lucknow, lunch at Fyzabad and dinner at Gaya.

I had expected to continue to Gauhati by the same route as the one I had taken a month before; that was the Eastern Bengal's Broad Gauge Assam Mail to Parbatipur, the same Railway's Metre Gauge Mail overnight to the ferry station of Amingaon and, after breakfast on the ferry, a short run of some five miles from Pandu to Gauhati. However, the severe monsoon, that had prevented the Japanese from following Burma Army into India, had played havoc with the Eastern Bengal's metre gauge line to Amingaon. The hill rivers and streams rushing down from the Himalayas, on reaching the flat plains of northern Assam, had run amok, washing out many miles of line; in fact, this line was not re-opened for about two months. I was advised to travel "south about" taking the Surma Mail from Calcutta to Goalundo Ghat, then a sail in a river steamer down the Padma, the estuary of the combined Ganges and Brahmaputra rivers, to the river port of Chandpur in Eastern Bengal. From there the Assam

Bengal's metre gauge Mail would take me to Badurpur Junction in south Assam, there I should have to change into a local "passenger" to travel over the scenic "Hill section" to Lumding, and change again into a local train for Gauhati. This journey would take forty eight hours instead of twenty four by the direct route.

The greater part of the journey was comfortable and of considerable interest. I noticed that there were no permanent station buildings at Goalundo; the station offices were located on a "flat" moored alongside the river bank and serving also as the steamer jetty. There was a good reason for this; the rivers in eastern India had a habit of eroding their banks when in spate, and retreating a very considerable distance when the river was low. The railway's modus operandi was to site the engine sheds some distance from the river where the main line locomotives were taken off, and then to propel the trains down to the waters edge with shunting engines, If the river either advanced or retreated, all that had to be done was to re-moor the flats and take up or extend the rails. I was to travel this route a number of times when, two years later, I was working in 14th Army Headquarters in Eastern Bengal, and I will always remember the quiet and comfortable sail down the Padma on a river steamer. These paddle steamers were operated by a British Company, the Indian General Steam Navigation Company, and were kept in immaculate condition. They were side paddlers, although a few old stern wheelers were still in service, carrying third class deck passengers on the lower deck and first and second class on the upper. The first class accomodation was forward consisting of a saloon flanked by cabins and a deck with long chairs over the bows. It was very pleasant to get on board after the grimy train fron Calcutta, enjoy an excellent curry lunch, take a siesta, and then lounge in a long chair and enjoy the river until dinner time. Chandpur was reached after dinner and the metre gauge mail left about 10 pm and reached Badurpur Junction in time for breakfast. I changed here into the Lumding passenger and had a thrilling ride over the mountains climbing up from near sea level to 6000 feet and down again to Lumding, which was reached in the evening. Once again after a somewhat chaotic journey, travelling third class I finally reached Gauhati next morning.

The security position in Assam was not unlike that which I had experienced earlier in Iraq and Burma – everything had to be started again from scratch as there were no such things as Officers Identity Cards or Field Security Warrant Cards, and practically no Field Security personnel. India did not issue Identity Cards until the winter of 1942/3, but we had the Warrant Cards printed by the Government Security Press in Calcutta and paid for out of the Secret Service funds. There was an all British Field Security Section which had come from Britain with HQ 4 Corps, and with the welcome arrival in Assam of two of my Burma Sections reasonable security cover was soon organised.

Assam was the "Cinderella" of the Provinces of British India – the smallest, the poorest and the most backward. Communications were very poor as there were only two tarred roads in the whole province, both "gated" hill roads which could only take traffic in one direction at a time – these were the Gauhati-Shillong-Sylhet road and the Manipur Road-Imphal road: the former did connect at Gauhati with the recently opened Assam Trunk Road, a dirt road running the whole length of the Assam valley from Gauhati to Dibrugarh, and in the south with a road to Silchar, but the other road was merely a feeder to the railway with no road connection onwards. There was no road connection at all with India proper, and the Brahmaputra was unbridged the whole of its length, but there was one railway wagon ferry in Assam and one in Bengal. The Province was split by the 6000ft high Khasi Hills into the the Surma Valley to the south and the Assam Valley to the north with the latter being further bisected by the Brahmmaputra. This river was navigable as far as Dibrugarh in the north east, and until the turn of the century provided the only through communication with Calcutta, although services could be erratic owing to low water in the summer and spates during the monsoon.

The railways serving the province and eastern Bengal, that is the part of Bengal lying to the east of the Padma, were the Assam Bengal, the Dibru Sadiya, and a small portion of the metre gauge section of the Eastern Bengal. In actual fact, the operating contract of the Assam Bengal was terminated in mid 1942, and this railway was taken into State operation and amalgamated with the state operated Eastern Bengal as the Bengal and Assam Railway. There was little change in operating methods for the time being and for clarity I will deal with the systems separately.

The main object of the promotion of railways in Assam was to provide a direct outlet on the Bay of Bengal and obviate the cumbersome route by river to Calcutta. The first railway in the Province, however, was the Dibru Sadiya, of only 60 miles, constructed by the Assam Railways and Trading Company to bring the coal and timber from the Ledo and Margherita area to the river port of Dibrugarh; this line later served the Digboi Oilfield. The Government of India, in 1891, started a line intended to connect the north east of Assam to the east Bengal port of Chittagong, but tired of the idea and handed over the project to a British private company, the Assam Bengal Railway Company Ltd. The whole line from Tinsukia Junction on the Dibru Sadiya to Chittagong was completed in 1904, the major obstacle being the section between Lumding and Badurpur Junctions where the line had to be taken over the mountains between the Assam and Surma valleys. This "hill section", of 120 miles, had to climb to over 6000ft with a ruling gradient of 1 in 37, and inumerable tunnels, bridges and sharp curves.

The main line started at Tinsukia Junction on the Dibru Sadiya and ran west roughly parallel to the Brahmaputra through the tea garden area of north east Assam. Near Jorhat it turned south west into a narrow valley, between the Regma Hills and the main mountain range of the Naga Hills, to reach Lumding Junction. The main station on this section was Manipur Road, situated at Dimapur, which was the road head for Kohima and Inphal, the capital of Manipur State. Lumding was also the junction for the Gauhati Branch, completed in 1892, although the five mile extension to the ferry port of Pandu was not opened until 1912, when the Eastern Bengal's branch arrived and set up a wagon ferry on the north bank at Amingaon. Gauhati was the northern road head for the provincial capital, Shillong.

The main line turned south at Lumding to cross, by the "hill section", the North Cachar Hills reaching an elevation of over 6,000 ft at Haflong Hill, before descending to almost sea level at Badurpur Junction, where there was a short branch to Silchar, the centre of a tea growing district. The line now ran due west through Sylhet District, with a branch to Sylhet Town, the southern road head for Shillong, and shortly afterwards passed out of Assam into Bengal. There were two important branches on the final section – one to Mymensing and Dacca on the Eastern Bengal's isolated metre gauge section and the other to the river port of Chandpur. The line was now in a jute growing area up to the terminus at the major sea port of Chittagong, where the Headquarters and Workshops of the Railway were located. The Assam Bengal had only two claims to fame – it operated, in its Assam Mail, the slowest express train in India, rather below 20 mph, and it operated, also on the Mail, one of the three Restaurant Cars then running on the metre gauge in the whole of India.

All these railways were of single line and, in general, of a low carrying capacity and rudimentary signalling. This caused considerable difficulties in supplying the troops facing the Japanese. The Port of Chittagong could not be used as the Japanese had command of the sea in the Bay of Bengal. Everything, therefore, had to come by metre gauge line over one or other of the wagon ferries and in the case of the southern route over the "hill section" also, with its major operating difficulties. Even before my return to Assam, it had become obvious that the railways were quite incapable of handling the military traffic – troops and stores inwards and the remnants of the Burma and Chinese Armies ouwards – to say nothing of the export of tea and the movement of petroleum products from the Digboi Field. An invasion of India from Burma had never been envisaged so the mobilisation plans for her defence had been concentrated on the North West where there was a network of strategic rail and road links – the railways were mainly broad gauge with an artificially high carrying capacity, as any operating loss was met from the Defence Budget. By contrast, communications in the North East were tailored to what was economically justifiable. To remedy this, measures were initiated to improve the wagon ferries and to increase the line capacity by the provision of extra passing loops.

Before anything had been achieved, fate dealt us two blows – the exceptionally severe monsoon floods washing out the north bank line and the dislocation and sabotage resulting from the severe civil disturbances known as the "1942 Rebellion". We were mercifully spared the very severe rioting which severed all three rail routes between Calcutta and the rest of India, but we did have two cases of attacks on repair gangs. These were not very severe in themselves but it meant the diversion of troops from other tasks. The wrecking of trains which started in the autumn of this year was a far greater problem. The modus operandi was extremely simple, and the only tool required was a long handled spanner, which could be stolen from railway stores or manufactured by any blacksmith. The wreckers would merely remove one or more fishplates, usually on a curve and the centrifugal force generated by the trains would distort the track and derailment followed.

The local Politicians and Press tried to maintain that these derailments were not caused by sabotage but were the result of excessive traffic and poor maintenance due to the War. There was an ulterior motive in this – first it was a good stick with which to beat the Government, but second and more inmportant, no compensation was payable to the victims, unless the Railway was proved at fault. The Railway administration denied this, and I was able to produce definate evidence of sabotage. A troop train had been derailed on a curve near Gauhati and the locomotive and the first two vehicles had gone down the embankment – luckily the loss of life was small as the two wrecked vehicles were luggage vans. The engine crew had been killed, the engine rolling over the Driver, and also two soldiers in the vans. I took a FS party to the scene, and sent them to search the undergrowth in the vicinity for clues, and our luck was in, as we recovered the fish plate, and better still a bolt which a tidy minded saboteur had put through the the fishplate hole, threading on the nut, before chucking the whole into the undergrowth. It was obvious that something had to be done, as the situation was aggravated by the desperate shortage of locmotives and rolling stock; often the Railway Officers had to make the agonising decision as to whether to roll everything off the track and resume operations, or to close it for several days while the stock and, particularily, the locomotive were recovered, often from the bottom of a high embankment.

The problem was daunting – there was nearly 700 miles of track in the Province used by military or essential traffic – the patrolling by railway permanent way gangs and the civil police was inadequate and the former were liable to be terrorised. The force which would have been used in normal times, the para military Assam Rifles, was not available as the bulk of them were patrolling the Burma border against Japanese infiltrators. On examination, however, the problem was not quite as bad as had been first thought – the main risk was in jungle areas were villages were few and the line abounded in sharp curves. The line from Pandu Ferry through Lumding to Manipur Road, about 250 miles, fell into this category as did the 185 miles of the "Hill Section", but here the risk was not so great as the line ran through tribal territory and any stranger would be spotted immediately by the Naga tribesmen, who had already been organised into the "North Cachar Watch and Ward" by a lady anthropologist, Miss Ursula Graham Bower. The two remaining sections were in areas of cultivation where villages and tea gardens were numerous.

The final solution was a three tier system. At the bottom of the scale were the villagers who were ordered, under threat of collective fines, to patrol the line in their vicinity, Above this was a force of Special Police recruited from locally domiciled Gurkhas – this force could be put together quickly as the men were merely given khaki shirts and shorts, army boots and a rifle with ten rounds in their pockets; the inevitable kukri the man provided himself. They, code name "Railforce", had detachments at most stations and patrolled the line checking the work of the villagers. The final tier, Railtroops, was an Indian Territorial Battalion, with its HQ and one company at Lumding and other companies at

Gauhati, Tinsukia, and Badurpur; the Commanding Officer was responsible for the whole scheme.

There were other facets of railway security – one was the morale of the train crews. Here we were lucky that most of the drivers and many of the firemen were Anglo Indians, and members of Assam Bengal Railway Battalion of the Auxiliary Force; they were extremely stout hearted and we never had any cases of crews refusing to take trains out at night.

Sabotage of the track and the consequent train wrecking was not the only possible form of sabotage – the destruction of stations, signal boxes and signalling equipment was also possible. The extent of dislocation was in inverse ratio to the sophistication of the signalling system – the railways in Assam, in general, had the lowest form of signalling equipment; the block system was worked in the main by telegraphic enquiry rather than by block token instruments, and at many of the crossing stations, the signals and points were not grouped into an interlocked frame, but were worked individually by hand levers. Should the telegraph be interrupted or the signals or points damaged, it was a simple matter to repair them. There were three areas, however,where things were very different – the Assam Bengal administration had resignalled Lumding and Badurpur Yards with colour light signals and electric point motors, worked from a signal box equipped with an electrically interlocked frame and, additionally, had equipped the crossing stations from Lumding to Manipur Road with a complicated interlocked double wire system of points and signals. Both these systems were a saboteur's dream – any damage to the signal boxes or the station double wire frames would halt all movement and this could only be resumed by the laborious method of unbolting the points, moving them over by hand and rebolting; enemy bombing, even a near miss, could have the same effect – this had happened at Myohoung in Burma (see Chapter V). Equally vulnerable were the power houses at Lumding and Badurpur. I happened to be in the Lumding signal box when there was a black out and, during the half hour before power was restored, all movement came to a halt. We were lucky that no attempt was made on these installations either by sabotage or bombing.

The morale of the railway employees, together with the evils of corruption and pilfering, also played a part and two incidents occurred during my early days in Assam. It was reported that a shunting engine had exploded in Pandu Yard, killing the crew and the other crews were refusing duty as they suspected that bombs were hidden in the coal. Any hold up in the movement of supplies forward was extremely serious, so I went myself to investigate. Things, luckily, were not as they had been reported – the engine had not blown up, merely an explosion had wrecked the cab and thrown the crew a considerable distance, so an explosion caused by a bomb in the coal was unlikley. A search of the area revealed remnants of a packing case in the vicinity and a wagon broken into. This wagon contained blasting powder, so it was obvious that the deceased had stolen a case, expecting it to contain tinned food, opened it on the footplate and a spark from the firebox had set it off.

The second case was a brush with the newly arrived Deputy General Manager for Assam of the B & A Railway. After the amalgamation of the E.B. and A.B. Railways, it was realised that the Assam lines could not be managed efficiently from Calcutta so a senior E.B. Officer, Mr Hussain, had been posted to Gauhati to manage the Assam lines from there. It was essential that Railtroops patrol various parts of the line at random, and the problem was – how would they get to and from the patrol areas. There were only two passenger trains on most of the line and of these the Mail only stopped at the principal stations. I requested permission, therefore, for the patrols to stop and then travel on goods trains during their patrols. This caused consternation among the train crews who looked upon it as attempt to stop their pilfering. They told a cock and bull story of the possible delay to movement and Mr Hussain, new to the ways of railways in Assam swallowed it. He said to me "Of course, Major, you do not understand railway working – the goods train would have to be halted at the station's outer home signal, and again at the home signal before stopping at the station, and the delay would be intolerable". I was flabbergasted – as if any goods train ever kept time, certainly the passenger trains never did. I replied, "But Mr Hussain, this might be so on a completely interlocked section of the Eastern Bengal, but here on the Assam Bengal, the Gauhati branch is Class 3 signalled without even starting signals and even the Mail may not run through at more than 5 mph as the Driver has to look out for the token for the section ahead, and to be ready to stop if necessary". Mr Hussain replied "I see, Major, that you know too much about railway operation", and issued the necessary orders. He was very helpful from then on issuing orders for all railway personnel to give me every assistance and also in giving the Gauhati Intelligence Detachment three 1st Class passes for the whole of Assam and to Calcutta. The latter I found very useful when I went on leave.

After the scheme had got under way I considered that I should go out "on line" and see how it was working and this could be combined with an inspection of the FS Sections at Manipur Road and Silchar. The two FS Officers concerned were old friends as they had commanded sections on the Burma Retreat. It was obvious that travel by ordinary train would not fulfill the first object, so I approached the District Traffic Superintendent at Pandu to lend me an Officers Saloon, which had the advantage that it could be attached to any train, passenger or goods and stop where and when I pleased, and he very kindly produced a four wheeled saloon. This was an Eastern Bengal vehicle in rather better condition and longer than the Assam Bengal saloons; the extra length was due to a very long rigid wheelbase. I loaded myself and my Gurkha orderly into the saloon and set off for Manipur Road, duly inspecting the security patrols on the way. I then back tracked to Lumding and over the "hill section" en route to Silchar. Nothing untoward occurred on this journey although I noticed that my saloon's wheels were grinding the rails fairly hard on the curves.

I intended to return to Lumding on my way home, and the saloon was attached at Badurpur to the rear of the daily passenger. Just before departure it was detached and the train departed without me; the Train Examiner then came and said that the saloon was "unfit to run" and, on being pressed for a

Bridge on Raipur Vizianagaram section, Bengal Nagpur Railway.

Lucknow Railway Station.

Parsik Tunnel between Bombay and Kalyan, G.I.P. Railway. The longest tunnel in present-day India.

Typical Indian Railway Signals.

reason, said that the wheelbase was too long for the curves on the hill section. My protests that it had arrived without mishap were of no avail and I was told to see the local District Traffic Superintendent, who happened to be in his office together with the District Mechanical Engineer. The former was inclined to be unhelpful and abide by the letter of the law, but I stressed that my sole object in undertaking this tour was to safeguard their railway, also that the saloon's loan had been very much on the "old boy net", and if it had to be worked back by a detour of a hundred miles or more and over two wagon ferries, Head Office in Calcutta would want to know about it, with possible adverse consequences for my friend at Pandu. The D.M.E then said – that while they could not risk a derailment in a tunnel, was the risk so very great as the saloon had come over without mishap. The D.T.S's attitude now softened and he agreed to let the saloon go back provided it was attached behind a goods train sandwiched between two manned brake vans.

I made one more trip in a saloon, this time to Dibrugarh in an extremely decrepit A.B. vehicle which rocked and creaked so much that I thought it was going to disintegrate at any minute, but the only mishap was the engine running short of water, causing the fire to be thrown out on the line with the consequent considerable delay. My main object on this occasion was to discuss, with the Sub Area H.Q and the local police, the ill behaviour of some of the American service men in the area. It was unfortunate that the Assam Government Distillery was situated adjacent to one of the U.S.A.A.F. Airfields, and this distillery produced the most frightful "hooch", locally known as "Dikom Death". Cases were constantly occuring of U.S. troops assaulting railway crews and also of raping female tea garden labour. A typical extract from a police report might read – "a drunken American soldier climbed onto the roof of a Dibrugrh-Tinsukia train, continued along the carriage roofs until he reached the engine where he assaulted the driver; the train then stopped". The local police were at first in awe of them, but their Superintendent soon got their measure. He told his constables that the U.S. troops were not to be treated like the

British planters, that is as Sahibs – but should they find a drunken American making a nuisance of himself, they were not to tackle him single handed, but to get reinforcements and then to hit him with their lathis until he became insensible and finally to send for the American M.P.s to take him away. I wondered how the U.S authorities would react to this, but I was told that they were happy as this was the way their M.Ps treated their drunks.

My time in Assam ended in the autumn of 1943 on being appointed to head the Security sub section of HQ XIV Army then being formed at Barrackpore near Calcutta. This meant that I should be responsible for security on 4 and 15 Corps fronts, as well as on the L of C in Assam and Eastern Bengal. Army HQ was to remain in Barrackpore for about a month, before moving to Comilla on the A.B. main line about half way between Chittagong and the Assam border. Barrackpore was only thirty minutes from Calcutta with a frequent suburban train service, making it possible to get into town after work and also to spend the night there, as a train leaving shortly after eight in the morning would get one to office by nine o'clock.

The Headquarters moved to Comilla via Goalundo and Chandpur in two special trains and steamers, and this journey served to illustrate the state into which the railways had fallen. We arrived at Chandpur in the evening and, as was usual in eastern India, there was no lighting in our train as all the bulbs had been stolen. I went alomg the carriages and warned all Officers to make sure that they fastened their window shutters against thieves, particularily as the lack of lighting would make theft more easy. The majority of these Officers had only recently arrived in India and I was told in no uncertain terms that nothing would induce them to shut the windows on a hot and sticky night. Next morning we came to a halt not far from Comilla, and on looking out, I was amused to see a number of Officers running up and down the train trying to borrow shirts and slacks as theirs had been stolen.

My work in an Army HQ was now very different as I was no longer directly concerned with security work, but had become, as a Staff Officer, a co-ordinator rather than an originator. I did practically no touring and thus, except for one rail trip to Chittagong, my rail journeys were only to and from Calcutta. I had to attend the monthly security conference of the military and police intelligence organisations of Assam, Bengal, Bihar and Orissa, together with the Special Branch of the Calcutta Police. This gave me a break of several days each month as I brought with me the XIV Army's monthly Security Summary to be printed at the Government of Bengal's Security Press, and took it back with me on my return. At first, I travelled both ways by air, but later the R.A.F. objected to the weight of several sacks containing the Summaries so, to my great satisfaction, I had to return by rail and steamer.

The Security Section's main concern with the Railways at this time was with the morale of the staff and its effect on the war effort, and with corruption and pilfering, which also was beginning to have an adverse effect. A job on the railways pre-war was much sought after, and indeed railway service had almost become a caste, as sons expected to be able to follow their fathers into the service. This had produced a pride in the job and in their particular Railway, not unlike that prevailing on British lines in the late Victorian era. Morale had started to decline in 1942, and by 1944 was at a very low level, particularily on the B & A; the Anglo Indian staff continued to work reasonably well, but the Indian railwayman's heart was not in his job. He could not be wholly blamed for this as he was no longer in a safe and well paid job with reasonable hours; instead he was having to work long hours, often in dangerous circumstances, and his pay had become utterly inadequate to keep him and his family. The position was aggravated by the phenomenal rise in food prices brought about shortages due to the Bengal Famine; all this he blamed on the War, so he was not prepared to make any further sacrifices for the war effort.

It was decided to partially militarise the B & A Railway by inviting the Indian staff to enlist in the "Defence of India" Regiment. They would then receive Army rations free, but would not be under military discipline, except that they could be punished if they deserted their posts. The Anglo Indian staff were already partly militarised by belonging to a railway unit of the Auxiliary Force. This measure went a long way to improve matters, but in some areas was not a complete success; a Station Master, as a senior railway employee could usually hold his own in an argument with a senior Army Officer, but was at a disadvantage when uniformed as a Second Lieutenant. The menial staff received their uniforms with gratitude and then wore them when going about their often dirty jobs; the sight of a man in a filthy shirt worn outside equally filthy shorts but with a military side cap and "D of I" shoulder titles did not enhance the reputation of the Indian Army among British and American soldiers.

The next move to speed up movement was to hand over operation of the metre gauge section from Partabipur Junction to Tinsukia, includung the Amingaon-Pandu wagon ferry, together with the D.S. Railway to the U.S. Army Transportation Troops. The local staff would remain but be subject to American orders, station masters would continue to deal with civilian passenger and goods traffic, but an American "Dispatcher" would be assigned to every station to oversee the work of the Indian staff. The local staff would continue to crew ordinary trains, but as far as possible all military specials, passenger or goods would be crewed by the Americans. This naturally caused a furore as the Americans troops behaviour towards the local population was often neither correct nor benevolent.

I was invited to a very high powered conference held in Calcutta between the British and American transportation agencies, the B & A Railway and the Security services and Police. The object was to ascertain the reaction of the Indian staff to this move and their main protagonist was Cuffe, the General Manager of the B & A. He was familiar with the area as before going, as General Manager, to the prestigious BB & CI Railway, he had been General Manager of the Assam Bengal. He was extremely efficient, but had the reputation of not suffering fools gladly; in fact his transfer to the B & A had caused some heart searching. Both the British and American Transportation representatives were extremely pessimistic, but Cuffe clinched the matter by saying that he thought that a someone in each station fully committed to the war effort might well raise the morale of the Indian staff. The scheme was a success, but there was a certain amount of anti American feeling amongst British Officers; it was unfortunate that the wreckage of the previous sabotage derailments was still lying beside the line and ill natured stories were current that this was due to accidents caused by recklessness on the part of the Americans.

Many readers will wonder why an Officer of the General Staff (Intelligence) should have to concern himself with corruption and pilfering, or downright robbery as it had become by 1944. Surely these were matters for the Civil Police or the Special Investigation Branch of the Military Police and they should have been, but unfortunately the Indian Police were neither interested, nor had the manpower, and in the lower ranks were corrupt themselves. The Military Police did not have the manpower either; pre war no members of the (British) Corps of Military Police served in India and provost work in cantonments was carried out by Garrison Military Police, the personnel, British and Indian, being provided by the units in garrison. A few British Provost units started to arrive in India from 1942, but these were usually part of British formations; a Corps of Indian Military Police was raised in mid 1942, but by autumn 1944 provost cover on the L of C was still very meagre and, up to that time, there were no S.I.B. personnel. By way of contrast, Security cover in eastern India was very wide; there were twenty four F.S. sections in XIV Army's area alone giving complete cover on the L of C from Dibrugarh to Chittagong. The F.S were not supposed to get involved in such matters, but often a house search for Intelligence reasons would disclose stolen rations, and there were no M.Ps to hand the case over to. An Indian was detained at a routine FS check at the Pandu ferry because he had an exceptionally heavy tin suitcase, and it was known that Japanese agents were equipped with such suitcases with built in radios. On being opened it was found to be full of bottles of whisky; the owner, a civilian canteen employee was arrested, but as there were no M.Ps the FS section had to take him under escort to Shillong and hand him over to H.Q. 251 L of C Sub Area.

There was no doubt that corruption existed in pre war days, but as those at the top were uncorrupt it was kept within bounds; such things as the rupee paid to the doorkeeper of the District Magistrate's Court, or the commission paid to one's Cook by the bazaar shopkeepers were well known and accepted. Indians, in general, were not thieves, and were extremely careful of any public or private property consigned to their care, but by 1944 all had changed – the shortage of everything from foodstuffs to railway wagons, the black market, and the lax climate brought about by the war and the influx of large numbers of British and American soldiers changed all this. There is no doubt that the theft of light bulbs and fans from railway carriages started with British soldiers, and as soon as the railway administration issued a Press Note that they could no longer guarantee lights in carriages, the Indian staff removed any which were left. The same happened in other theatres of war, in fact, robbery on the L of C in Europe probably greatly exceeded anything in India. It was serious, however, as owing to the lack of roads everything had to be sent by rail, and thus had to be escorted or the wagon might never start on its journey at all, or be broken into en route, and the provision of escorts was a great waste of manpower.

One day in Comilla, the R.A.F Security Liason Officer came to me in a great state of excitement saying that a complete wagon load of Spitfire spares had been lost between Calcutta and Chittagong; he was inclined to attribute this to sabotage as the spares were for the first such Squadron to arrive in India, and the enemy were attempting to immobilise it. I asked him if the R.A.F had sent an escort with the wagon; he looked amazed and said – no, they had locked and sealed it, booked it with the Railway Transport Officer and here was the Waybill to support it. I was aghast at the folly of these proceedings and asked him, with some asperity, if he thought that any Station or Yard Master on the B & A Railway would forward his wagon if he could get one hundred Rupees for forwarding a private trader's wagon. I then assured him that we would find his wagon and instituted a search by the F.S. from each end. It was found about eighty miles from Calcutta and there it might have remained until the end of the war. It was lucky that it had only gone that far, as without an escort, it would have been extensively pilfered while being reloaded on transhipment from broad to metre gauge.

The British clerks in the R.T.O's Office at Calcutta's Sealdah Station, in conjunction with the railway's reservation staff, ran a flourishing racket over places on the daily Assam and Surma Mails. The modus operandi was to allot only a small percentage of the available places and fill up the remainder with fictitious names. Officers requiring reservations were told that the train was fully booked for some three or four days, but if they turned up at departure time the reservation babu might be able to fit them in. A few accepted the later booking but most, anxious to return to their units on time, accepted this advice, got a place and gratefully tipped the reservation babu, who split the takings with the R.T.O's staff. This usually led to a gross waste of space, as I well knew as I travelled on the Surma Mail each month after the Security Conference; of course, I had a priority certificate for accomodation. On one occasion, there were only two of us travelling in accomodation meant for twelve; the other traveller was the Deputy Director of Movements of XIV Army, who complained that he could not understand how this train was always reported as fully booked; I soon put him wise. I kept out of this because it was not an Intelligence matter, Calcutta was not in my jurisdiction and was one of the few places where there was adequate provost cover.

PART III
POST WAR JOURNEYS
1944–52.

CHAPTER VII

SNOW IN BALUCHISTAN – 1944–46.

I have taken chronological licence in placing this Chapter in "Post War Journeys", but the War did end during this period, and the North Western Railway was operating normally with none of the dislocations which I had found east of Calcutta. A Committee had been set up to study the morale of Indian soldiers after the Malayan and Burma debacles, and this had recommended that as many Regular Officers as possible should be returned to units; I was one of these and was posted as Second in Command of our latest raised Battalion, the 5th, stationed at Chaman on the Afghanistan border in Baluchistan. This involved me in almost the longest rail journey that it was possible to take within India, almost 2,400 miles, and as I was able to get a lift to Chandpur in an F.S. truck I arrived at my destination with a ticket headed "Indian Steam Navigation Co Ltd".

I travelled by the familiar route via Goalundo to Calcutta and, after a night there, continued onward by the East Indian's Punjab Mail to Lahore, or that was what I should have done, but instead decided to divert via my Regimental Centre at Dehra Dun and spend a couple of days there. Amenities improved as soon as Calcutta was passed; for one thing there were lights in the Mail's carriages. My knowledge of the Timetable told me that I should have to change trains at Lakhsar Junction in the middle of the night, so I left the Mail at Lucknow about tea time on the second day, had dinner there and picked up No 9 Doon Express in the evening. I left Dehra Dun on my onward journey by the through coach on the Delhi Express which was detached at Lakhsar and re-attached to the Punjab Mail arriving at Lahore in time for breakfast. The Karachi Mail which left at 9 am had a through coach for Quetta, which was transferred at Rohri to the Bolan Mail coming from Karachi. I was uncertain whether the Punjab Mail would arrive in time or whether I should be able to get a berth in the Quetta coach. This through coach was the most comfortable way for the ordinary traveller as the journey was only of 24 hours duration and the Karachi Mail had a Restaurant Car. I considered, however, that I would do better to go by the Quetta Pasenger, as I was more likely to get a coupé to myself on a less popular train.

The Quetta Passenger was typical of an all stations slow train, which ran for a very considerable distance on the North Western; it took about 40 hours to do the 700 miles at an average speed of about 17mph. After a sprint of 24 miles from Lahore to Raiwind without a stop, it settled down to stop at all stations right up to Quetta; not a popular train for the ordinary traveller. Meals were no problem for me, the Guard wired ahead and they were brought to my compartment – breakfast at Samasata, lunch at Khanpur, dinner at Rohri and breakfast on the second day at Mach, half way up the Bolan Pass. I found the journey fascinating, although the first day across the flat Punjabi plain was of little scenic interest; the North Western had doubled the main line from Karachi to Samasata before World War I in anticipation of a boom in wheat exports which never materialised, but had not equipped the Samasata-Rohri section with normal double line block instruments, using instead two single line token instrument for each block section. The second morning found the train just inside the Bolan Pass, interesting from both a scenic and operational point of view. A Regimental 3 ton lorry was waiting for me at Quetta as the Chaman local train only ran twice a week. I cannot remember the motive power from Lahore to Rohri, but up the Bolan Pass it was the HG 2–8–0, one in front and two banking.

The strategic lines of the North Western Railway were one of the most interesting areas both of railway development and of operation; they included the highest and longest tunnel in undivided India, and the second highest narrow gauge summit. They consisted of the main line from Jacobabad to Chaman, the secondary route through the Chappar Rift, the Nushki extension to Zahidan in Iran and the narrow gauge Zhob Valley line.

The Government of India, spurred on by the threat of war with Afghanistan, issued orders in 1876 for a railway to be constructed to Quetta, but this was not started until 1879, although a certain amount of flood prevention works were carried out. The reason for the delay was an argument as to whether it was be be a fair weather or an all weather line, but the appallimg difficulties experienced by troops and animal transport crossing the dreaded Kacch plain, caused a start to be made. The Kacch plain between Jacobabad in Upper Sind and Sibi at the foot of the Baluchistan mountains, is flat with a gradual descent towards Jacobabad of 1 in 2,000; in the summer, temperatures of 125°F have been recorded but in winter it freezes at night. A cloud burst in autumn in the Baluchistan mountains can send raging torrents across the plain sweeping everything away. Although the loss of life of men and animals crossing the plain had been heavy, except for the southern end, railway construction during the winter months posed few problems.

The southern end was the problem. The annual Indus floods had raised the level of Upper Sind and, where the Kacch plain met this slightly higher area of cultivation, a great depression had formed which was inundated annually by the Indus floods. It was to remedy this that three years had been spent in preventative measures, and in 1879, for the first time in living memory, the great embankment at Kashmor held and there were no floods. The Engineers took a chance and laid the line on the surface of the land only raising it sufficiently to cross the numerous irrigation channels. Their luck held right up to 1942, when the Indus burst through the embankment and put the line out of action for three months. The line known as the "Kandahar State Railway" was opened to Sibi in January 1880.

The engineers meanwhile had surveyed a line onwards following the old caravan route which had been improved into a road; this followed the Bolan River through the Kundilani Gorge and the Bolan Pass, but was rejected for a railway as the gradients would have been as severe as 1 in 25. A different route was found through the Chappar Rift which could reach rhe Quetta plateau with a ruling gradient of 1 in 44, but the project was shelved at the end of 1880 owing to the withdrawal of British troops from Afghanistan. It was re-started again in 1883 but to fit in with Gladstone's policy of peace and retrenchment, it was originally called the "Harnai Road Improvement Scheme", later known the "Sind-Pishin Railway".

The Chappar Rift line was one of the engineering wonders of the world. It penetrated the hills by running up the Nari Valley, crossing and re-crossing the dry river bed by innumerable bridges, it then entered the Rift, an incredible freak of nature, where the hills have literally split asunder, and by tunnelling and bridging reached the top, it then crossed a valley of dried mud, which after rain becomes a quagmire, to reach 6,533 ft, before dropping down and, in 1887, arriving at Quetta from the north, where another line had already entered from the south.

While the Chappar Rift line was under construction, the troops in Quetta had continued to be supplied by the Bolan Road, and to facilitate this a branch had been built from Sibi to Rindli in the foothills. It was decided in 1885 to build a fair weather line by this route and it was done simultaneously in three sections. The broad gauge line was extended from Rindli to Hirok at the entrance to the actual Bolan Pass, metre gauge thence to Kolpur at the suumit and broad gauge onward to Quetta which was reached in 1886; the rise from Sibi to Quetta is over 5,000 feet. The construction was of a very temporary nature, much of the line being laid on the dry river bed. The extension from Bostan Junction on the Chappar Rift line to Chaman on the Afghanistan border crossed the 8,000 to 9,000 ft Khwaja Amran range by the Khojak Tunnel and reached Chaman by 1890. This double line bore was the longest tunnel in undivided India and the summit of over 6,000 ft was the highest altitude reached by a broad gauge railway.

Meanwhile both the Chappar Rift direct line and the Bolan route were used from Sibi to Quetta. Neither was a success – the Chappar Rift was plagued by washouts, landslips and subsidences which in the six years from 1887 to 1893, interrupted through traffic on nineteen occasions – traffic was held up each time for anything from three days to three weeks. Traffic moved slowly on the Bolan route, with its two transhipments, and where, on the metre gauge, Fairlie double ended locomotives puffed laboriously up the 1 in 23 gradients. A new "high level line" on the Abt rack system had actually been constructed, when the floods of 1889 and 1890 washed this away before it had ever been opened.

The unsatisfactory nature of both routes caused the Government to think again, and a new route was surveyed – the "Mushkaf-Bolan" in use to this day. This line is taken up the Mushkaf valley for about twenty five miles and then by a tunnel into the Bolan valley, entering it about 200 feet above the valley floor. Thence an entirely new alighnment with a ruling gradient of 1 in 25 carried it up to Kolpur. This new route was opened in 1895.

The original section of the Kandahar State Railway ran due north from Jacobabad and is almost dead straight for ninety miles – an engine headlight can be seen for eighteen miles. Stations are merely block posts and, in the absense of villages, have been named after personnel working on the construction, examples are Nuttall and Lindsay. After Sibi, the line climbs steadily up the Mushkaf Valley on gradients of 1 in 53 to the tunnel; once into the Bolan Valley it drops down slightly to the station of Ab-i-gum. This is the start of the Bolan incline, the place where the banker is attached and the double line to Kolpur begins. The double line section was built for strategic reasons to speed up military traffic, particularily as the bankers have be worked back light engine. The next eight miles to Mach is at 1 in 33, and up trains overshoot the Station and have to reverse back into the yard, where a second banker is attached. The reason is that there is not sufficient level ground to accomodate the station and yard on one or other side of the mainline. Down trains run straight into the station, and proceeding onward have to reverse out and over to the down line before they can get away. The gradient onward is at 1 in 25 except for a short level stretch through Hirok station before it begins to ease to 1 in 35, followed by 1 in 40 into Kolpur; the section onward to Quetta is comparatively level.

The Chappar Rift line gradually wasted away; by the thirties all the through trains were running via the Bolan Pass, and the local service between Sibi and Quetta had shrunk to twice weekly. It remained open partly as a second route should the Bolan route be blocked and partly on account of the coal mines at Khost half way up the line. A cloud burst in July 1942 caused a washout in the

Rift and traffic was halted. Owing to the more serious flooding in Upper Sind and general preoccuption with the war effort, the damage was not fully assessed until the following year when the decision was taken to cut back to Khost and recover the material on the upper section. Thus ended one of the railway engineering marvels of the world.

The other broad gauge line was the 440 mile long Nushki Extension. The original section to Nushki was opened from Spezand Junction near Quetta in 1905, and extended across the desert to Zahidan, just inside Iran, between 1917 and 1922. By the thirties only the 219 miles to Nok-kundi was in use and much of the remainder had been dismantled. It was reconstructed in 1942 as one of the routes by which allied war material could reach Russia. The journey by the weekly passenger train took thirty eight hours at an average speed of 12 mph. The service was advertised as "conveying a Buffet car", which was, in fact, only a four wheeled goods vehicle selling Indian food.

The final railway in Baluchistan was the 2ft 6 narrow gauge Zhob Valley line. This was originally built from Khanai on the Chappar Rift line to some chrome mines in the mountains between the Pishin plateau and the Zhob Valley; opened in 1917, it was operated for goods only as an "assisted siding". It was converted to a railway and extended to Hindubagh (now Moslem Bagh) in 1921, and to Fort Sandeman (now known as Zhob) in 1927, and at the same time it was extended at the other end to Bostan Junction. The total length was 173 miles and the twice weekly train took about 15 hours for the journey. The first section to Hindubagh was over the mountains with severe gradients and the summit reached, 7,200 ft, was the second highest of any Indian railway as it was higher than Simla, and only just short of the summit of the Darjeeling Himalayan. The section onward was along the Zhob Valley, crossing the so called dry river beds by "Irish bridges" which could become impassable in the event of of heavy rain. It was also severely affected by climatic conditions – snow and frozen engines.

The original motive power on the Sind Pishin Railway were the "L" Class 4–6–0s. The first of these had been built for the Indus

100

Valley Railway in 1880, and the last in 1899. They were the first 4–6–0s in India and were similar to the first 4–6–0s on the (British) Highland Railway; they lasted on the Chappar Rift line until 1928. Later, except for a few "XA" Pacifics on the lightly laid and easily graded Zahidan line, the "HG" 2–8–0s were used for both passenger and goods trains and as bankers; the bankers had a headlight on the tender to enable them to work back tender first. Other locomotives were tried at different times – first some 2–8–2Ts and later both a Garratt and an American built 2–6–6–2 Mallet were used, but they were found to be less economical than two HGs. Ultimately one of the new "XG" Class 0–8–0s was tried as a banker, and also one of the "N" Class 2–10–0s, displaced by electrification from the GIP Ghat lines, but in the end nothing was found better than the ubiquitous "HG". The start of an up train from Mach was an experience. As soon as the two bankers had compressed the couplings, all three drivers yanked open their regulators and the train thundered out onto the 1 in 25 gradient

I did not do a great deal of travelling during my year in Baluchistan, and, to my regret I never travelled through the Shelabagh Tunnel to or from Quetta. As there were only two very slow trains a week, it was not possible to go into Quetta for a days shopping by train but the 120 miles round trip could easily be done by road over the Khojak Pass. The railway was our life line in winter, however, as the Pass was closed for several days by snow, but the railway going through the tunnel at a lower altitude remained open.

The station at Chaman was literally on the frontier, and near by were a number of sheds, which, rumour had it, contained the material to extend the line to Kandahar in the event of a fourth Afghan War. There was a heavy traffic in fruit brought by lorry from Kandahar, and dispatched onward in ice bunkered wagons, necessitating a daily special goods train. The supply of wagons was never adequate for the traffic offering, and the hubbub created by the arguments this engendered could be heard all over the cantonment. There is no doubt that the railway staff benefited greatly from this, and the story was current that the North Western Railway administration used to post a very senior

Station Master to Chaman to enrich himself in his last year of service.

The Shelabagh Tunnel was both difficult to construct and to operate; much of the bore was through treacherous water bearing strata for which Welsh miners, with experience of working on the Severn Tunnel, were imported to cope with the situation. The two and a half mile long tunnel has no ventilation shafts and is approached by a very long ramp up from Chaman, mostly at 1 in 40 which continues into the tunnel before easeing to 1 in 80, and further on to a short stretch of 1 in 500 before reaching the summit, where a treadle operated gong warned the enginemen to shut off steam. All trains were banked, often by two engines and cases occurred of the the train engine entering Shelabagh station braking, but with one or other of the bankers still steaming hard as the crew had become unconscious because of the fumes. We then had to send a military ambulance from Chaman.

The Battalion moved from Chaman to Fort Sandeman in the spring of 1945, and so I travelled on the Zhob valley line several times. My first journey inspired the title of this Chapter – "Snow in Baluchistan". My Commanding Officer suggested that before our move I should go and spend a weekend with the Brigade Major in Sandeman, who was a personal friend, and take a couple of Gurkha Officers with me to spy out the land. We set off in late February to catch the Friday train from Bostan, scheduled to arrive on Saturday morning, and return on the Monday evening. The Zhob trains were timed to connect with the trains to and from Quetta and not those from Chaman, so we went to Bostan over the Khojak Pass in a Regimental 3 tonner. The winter of 1944–5 was the coldest in living memory in northern India and Chaman was no exception – 0° F being recorded in the night, but by now it was much milder, almost spring like. We left on a cold sunny morning, but on reaching the top of the Pass, I noticed that the sky had become an angry purple. I had lunch in the station Refreshment Room, and set about organising tea and supper as there were no Refreshment Rooms en route; tea and toast, however, could be obtained from tea stalls at most stations, and we were scheduled to arrive in time for breakfast. I had an

102

extra large portion of scrambled eggs put into a hot food container and tea into a Thermos, plus several slices of bread and butter; a bottle of whisky completed my preparations. The upper class carriages on the narrow gauge were very comfortable – each contained two single berth I class compartments in the centre, and two double berth second class at the ends each with its own bathroom, but, of course, no heating . The low roof level meant that there were no upper berths and the water tanks were under the bathroom floors, water being obtained by individual rotary pumps.

We left at about 3 pm along the old Chappar Rift alignment to Khanai, where the 1 in 25 gradient began and immediately ran into a blizzard. Our motive power was three "G" Class 2–8–2s, one leading and two banking; the leading engine was fitted with a minature snow plough. Darkness fell and I lit a hurricane lamp and had my tea – we battled on almost at walking pace, and later I eat my scrambled egg and had a whisky or two. The cold was intense, so I decided that after supper the best thing was to go to bed; by now we had still not reached the summit although we were close to the time when we should have been changing engines at Hindubagh. In spite getting into my sleeping bag with all my clothes on, and with my greatcoat on top, I passed a cold and unpleasant night.

The next morning found us at Hindubagh, where tea and toast could be obtained and we did not get started again until about midday as all the engines were frozen up. There was a hope that we might reach Sandeman that evening, but just as dusk was falling the engine ran off the line. This was a minor mishap on the narrow gauge, where the locomotives carried jacks and other equipment to re-rail without outside assistance, but it did mean that our arrival time would now be mid morning on Sunday. This was annoying enough for me but more so for the other Officer passenger; he had been invited to a weekend shoot by the Political Agent and had already lost Saturdays's sport and looked like losing Sunday's also. Help was at hand as the P.A. had sent out a squad of the para military Zhob Militia to find his guest. They duly brought us into Sandeman by road in time for dinner. I had learnt my lesson – on all my subsequent journeys, I travelled with a Primus stove, kettle, frying pan and the wherewithal to cook a hot supper, and breakfast as well if the train was likely to be very late.

I had several trouble free journeys, happy with my arrangements to provide meals as and when I wanted them, but I had problems on my last journey – in June I was given two months leave to England and ordered to report at Karachi for an air passage. It had been raining heavily on the day of my departure, but had cleared by the evening. The Bostan train was ready to start, but the Station Master had taken the precaution of sending out a trolley to check that the "Irish bridges" were passable. It had just returned with the all clear, when a cloud burst occurred and there was nothing for it but go home and return on the following morning. This time we got away, but it was quite an experience when the train went down into the river beds with the water reaching up to the carriage footboards.

My return from leave had to be by troopship as, owing to the Japanese surrender, the air passages were fully booked, and it did not arrive at Bombay until early December. Our party were mostly regular Officers – C.O.s and Seconds in Command – and to speed up our return, we had been issued before departure with railway warrants from Karachi to our units. These were not recognised by the Bombay Movements Staff who packed us off to a horrible transit camp at Kalyan, where the final indignity was the free issue of mosquito nets "on first arrival in India". A few days later I was put on a "Special Military Express" for Lahore. These trains were run to prevent overcrowding by military personnel of the ordinary mail and express trains. The accomodation provided was in either the oldest upper class coaches that could be found or in "Special Military Cars" a slightly more comfortable version of the Military Cars described in Chapter III. These trains were slow, never kept time, and the feeding arrangements were chaotic – the result was that Officers used every subterfuge to avoid them. This type of travel soon got under my skin so when we reached Amballa I detrained and took a cross country train via Patiala and Bhatinda to Samasata where

I picked up my old friend the Quetta Passenger. All this was entirely against orders, but I had a very pleasant and comfortable journey. On arrival at Quetta I reported to the R.T.O. for onward conveyance to Fort Sandeman. To my horror I found that my unit had moved to Wana in South Waziristan; they had notified the R.T.O at Lahore to re-direct me but, of course, having by passed that place, the message did not reach me.

There was nothing to be done but get a berth in the Lahore through coach on that evenimg's Mail, detrain at Multan, trundle up the left bank of the Indus in a slow Passenger to Darya Khan on the Sind Sagar Doab Railway, from where I could get by road to Dera Ismail Khan, and onward to Manzai, the gateway to South Waziristan. The Sind Sagar Doab line was a strategic lateral down the east bank of the Indus from Campbellpore to Multan giving access to all the Frontier towns and garrisons south of Peshawar – Jand Junction for the broad gauge line to Kohat, Mari Indus for the narrow gauge to Bannu and Tank, Darya Khan for the bridge of boats to Dera Ismail Khan and finally Ghazi Ghat for the ferry to Dera Ghazi Khan. I had to wait in the transit quarters at Manzai for a "R.O.D" – a road open day – when the road was picketed by the local South Waziristan Scouts and a heavily escorted convoy left for Wana. I suppose I should have had a reprimand for my unauthorised diversion and the extra expense caused to Government, but nothing happened, and anyway the extra rail journeys were well worth it.

'L' class 4–6–0.   *P.S.A. Berridge. MBE, MICE*

'N' class 2–10–0.

P.S.A. Berridge. MBE, MICE

'Mallet' 2–6–6–2.

P.S.A. Berridge. MBE, MICE

Narrow Gauge 'G' class Zhob Valley Line with miniature snow plough fitted.
P.S.A. Berridge. MBE, MICE

Locomotive XGM 2-8-0.   *P.S.A. Berridge. MBE, MICE*

The Chappar Rift. *P.S.A. Berridge. MBE, MICE*

At the upper or Mangi end, the jig-saw puzzle like fit of the two sides of the Chappar Rift shows how the mountain was split open in an earthquake. The flood waters which breached the line and closed the railway for all time rose to a height of 30 feet at the narrow entrance to the chasm. *P.S.A. Berridge. MBE, MICE*

Three HG/S 2-8-0s rush 53 up Lahore-Quetta passenger across bridge No 198 over the Nannar Nala at the start of the 13-mile climb up through the Bolan Pass.

P.S.A. Berridge. MBE, MICE

CHAPTER VIII

A PERIOD OF UNCERTAINTY – 1946-7

A month and a half after my arrival in Wana, I was posted as Chief Intelligence Officer at HQ Central Command in Agra and set off by an R.O.D for Manzai. This time I was the convoy Commander and as a result had a more comfortable journey than on the way up. During my wait for the bi-weekly train, I was given the V.I.P. transit quarter, and also allowed to sleep in the train on the night before the 4 am departure. Manzai was inside tribal territory and therefore the station was inside the perimeter wire. Trains arriving had to halt outside, and all passengers, other than military personnel, had to detrain – the train was then searched before the gate in the wire was opened and it was allowed in. The journey to Agra took about 28 hours, but this included an eight hour wait at Lahore – narrow gauge to Mari Indus and broad gauge onward via Lahore and Delhi. The train from Lahore to Agra was the GIP's Punjab Mail, which continued onward from Delhi to Lahore over the North Western's Southern Punjab Railway – that is via Ferozepore and Bhatinda and requiring a reversal at Delhi Junction.

The area for which I was to be responsible was enormous – half of the Punjab, that was all south of the Ravi River and including Lahore, the United Provinces and the Central Provinces with a number of Native States thrown in for good measure. It was equivalent in size to France and Benelux and had a population of some 60 million. Part of the main lines of four railways were included in it – the North Western, the East Indian, the GIP and the BB & CI, to say nothing of the metre gauge main line of the latter and the metre gauge lines of the Oudh and Rohillakund and the Bengal and North Western Railways radiating from Lucknow. The Indian Railways were recovering slowly from the doldrums of 1942, when Wavell, as Commander in Chief, had demanded a minimum of 185 broad gauge locomotives and had been told curtly that he could have 5. The Americans were the first to realise the parlous condition of the railways in eastern

India and, in late 1943, produced a few metre gauge 2–8–2s from American and Canadian builders, and a few similar broad gauge locomotives in the following year. The same year saw the repatriation, from the Middle East, of many of the Railway Construction and Operating Companies of the Royal Indian Engineers, this allowed a number of key routes to be improved and extra services run. By now a number of American and Canadian built broad gauge engines had arrived ; 2–8–0s of Class AWC and 2–8–2s of Classes AWD, CWD, and AWEs, togther with a number of metre gauge 2–8–2s, but the use of these was severely restricted owing to the very considerable mileage of lightly laid track.

Central Command was made up of three military "Areas" with HQs at Lahore, Lucknow and Nagpur, and Sub Area HQs at such places as Amballa, Dehra Dun, Meerut, Jubbulpore and Cawnpore to name but a few, and I was constantly on the move visiting them. Travel was more comfortable than it had been, but by no means back to pre war standards, but most of my journeys were short and often by cross country slow trains which were seldom overcrowded. Lucknow was a day time journey and I solved the accomodation problem on the Calcutta Mail by having lunch in the Restaurant Car, and then for a small tip getting the staff to allow me to remain there until my destination. Nagpur by the Grand Trunk Express was a longer journey; this train, which ranked as a Mail, had been put on in the early thirties to provide a through train from Delhi to Madras. It was not very fast as it traversed a number of branch lines with primative signalling, and, with the exception of the last few miles into Madras, ran the whole way on single lines. Its route was from Delhi to Itarsi by the GIP's Delhi main line, then over a cross country branch to Nagpur and a reversal, back down the GIPs Nagpur main line to Wardha, the Nizam's State then worked it to Bezwada, from whence the M&SM took it to Madras over their north east main line.

I was in many ways my General's political adviser and as such was required to advise him as to whether the railways in our Command would be able to continue to function efficiently in the then adverse political climate. This included riot and disorder, both anti-Government and communal, and, for the first time for some years, labour unrest. These factors were loosely linked together by the general trend of nationalist aspirations. Strikes, although ostensibly for economic reasons, often had an undertone of political motivation, and the anti Government and communal riots, also, were linked to the political moves in the immediate pre-Independence period. The economic malaise of the staff which had manifested itself in eastern India during the proceeding years, had now spread to all railways and nothing short of a drastic improvement in pay and working conditions would have any effect.

Strikes did occur, but they were sporadic and usually of either a day or a few hours duration. They caused dislocation and discomfort to travellers, but did not bring all movement to a halt, as the Anglo Indian staff remained aloof as did a number of the Assistant Station Masters. A few strikes were accompagnied by disorder; on the North Western, unruly mobs endeavoured to stop traffic by disconnecting the vacuum brake hoses, just as the train was about to leave or by sitting on the track. At one time the North Western administration issued orders that trains should leave principal stations without the brake being connected and to stop at a wayside station to re-connect it. A nation wide railway strike was called in the summer of 1946, but called off so as not to embarrass the new popular interim Government. This, with serious rioting in many parts of the country, caused a greater or lesser degree of dislocation but the effect was not particularily severe, and the enormous size of the country left many areas untouched. I travelled extensively in the southern Punjab and in the U.P. in the summer of 1946 with no greater annoyance than an enforced wait of four hours at one station short of Saharanpur while travelling from Lucknow to Lahore. This was because the North Western signalman who controlled Saharanpur, was on strike and refused to give line clear for the East Indian's Punjab Mail.

Army HQ became a alarmed in the spring of 1946 at the unrest in the country and at the inflammatery speeches of the politicians

113

and ordered each Army Command to prepare plans to quell any uprising, using such force as might be necessary including armoured vehicles. It was obvious that, in such a situation, reliance could not be put on the railways, so the intelligence staff were put to work re-surveying the roads and in particular the bridges. The existing "route books" were out of date and envisaged the movement of marching columns of men and animals, and not M.T. or tanks on or off transporters. Some of the major bridges were dual, that is with the railway on the top deck and the road underneath. Blockhouses were incorporated at either end with gates which could be closed across both rail and road; these were manned in time of civil disturbance by the appropriate railway battalion of the Auxiliary Force. The problem was that the road entered the blockhouse at right angles and then had to do a 90° turn onto the bridge; while it was possible that a tank might be able to carry out this manoeuvre, it would be quite impossible for a transporter. The two roads to the south (the Bombay-Agra and the Cawnpore-Jhansi) were another problem; these crossed the Chambal River by bridges of boats which was replaced during the monsoon by a very inefficient manual ferries, which were suspended if the river was in spate. Luckily the adjacent railway bridges had been decked against an emergency. The G.I.P Railway administration looked upon the Army's use of these bridges as a great nuisance and were inclined to be unhelpful; for example the great bridge at Kalpi south of Cawnpore was a case in point. It was approached by long and high embankments and the railway authorities insisted that any road convoy be treated as a train, and as such, have to obtain the "line clear" token and carry a railway man on the first and last vehicle with lamps and flags to protect the line in the event of a halt.

My wife to be, Pauline, was introduced to Indian Railways when she arrived at Delhi in late September for our wedding at Agra. We went there by the Grand Trunk Express. Her first reaction was surprise at the size of a four berth compartment with its own lavatory and, then she was horrified, when after leaving New Delhi station, I opened the carriage door – Indian carriage doors opened inwards – so that she could have better view of New Delhi's Central Vista and the Viceroy's House. We went on leave to Kashmir shortly after the wedding and our journeys to and from the railhead at Jammu call for no comment.

On our return to Agra, I found that I had been selected to attend the Staff College course at Quetta; the problem was how best to get there. The official way was to take a Special Military Express from Agra to Lahore and then hope that the R.T.O. there could find us two berths in the Quetta through coach. I did not relish this as on both trains the possibility of getting a coupé to ourselves was remote and it was quite likely that we would be separated – Pauline in a Ladies' compartment and I in a Mens'. I suggested, therefore, that we went in the Punjab Mail from Agra to Lahore and then took my old friend the Quetta Passenger. We had a most comfortable journey, a coupé to ourselves and our meals brought to the compartment at the appropriate times. Prior to our own departure I had obtained a horsebox and sent off my horse with his groom, and also some of our kit and my pony trap duly broken down into its component parts. A horsebox would take six horses and the box was charged at the same rate irrespective of the number of horses or grooms travellimg, but only the animals' forage and the grooms' bedding rolls were carried free – any baggage or household goods loaded into the spare space had to be paid for. While unloading the box at Quetta, I was accosted by a ticket examiner who asked for my waybill and luggage ticket; I had, of course, to confess that I had only booked and paid for the vehicle, but I said politely that it was a bit unfair to have to pay extra, when the greater part of the horse box had not been used. He was very reasonable and let the luggage go free, but said that would have to charge for the pony trap. He relented somewhat by agreeing to weigh and charge only some parts as a gesture, but as these were being put onto his weighing machine he said – "No, Sahib, that is one of the heavier pieces, give me one of the lighter". I duly paid up and honour was satisfied all round.

Pauline and I did no travelling while we were at Quetta; I had intended to take her to Dehra Dun during our ten day "break", but the horrific tales of of conditions on and around Lahore station deterred us. Everything was now slowly slipping into chaos as Independence Day drew near. The old Government had issued instructions that, for the time being, everything would continue as before; trains would run across the Indo-Pakistan border according to the existing timetable, through bookings would continue and so on. This however proved to be a complete pipe dream.

Conditions on the North Western Railway soon deteriorated. The first difficulty was the transfer of staff – while only 5000 Moslem staff wished to transfer from India to Pakistan, 25000 Hindu and Sikh employees wished to move the other way; a situation that caused a serious staff shortage in Pakistan. Meanwhile a massive general exodus of Hindus and Sikhs started from Pakistan, and a slghtly smaller one in the opposite direction. No one knows who fired the first shot, but from Independence Day onwards the two communities were attacking each other in earnest; a situation beyond the capacity of the Army and Police to control. One of the greatest difficulties was the reluctance of the running staff to report for duty, even after military escorts were provided, as they did wish to leave their families unprotected. The North Western and its offshoot in India, the Eastern Punjab Railway, soon suspended all trans-frontier scheduled services, except for the Frontier Mail which carried mostly official passengers. On the 24th of August, the Mail arrived at Delhi 24 hours late, after having been attacked by 200 armed men, and on the same day the Government of West Punjab issued an official warning that rail travel between Lahore and Delhi was unsafe. Shortly after this, in early September, the Eastern Punjab Railway gave up the unequal struggle and suspended all scheduled passenger services to concentrate on the movement of troops, refugees, food grains and coal – the North Western alone required 3,000 tons a day, almost all of which had to come from eastern India. Much the same happened on the Lahore and Multan Divisions of the North Western, although passenger services of a sort were still running in Sind and Baluchistan.

Pauline and I had decided to extend our service in India, instead of transferring to the British Army, and, on the enforced conclusion of the Staff College Course in October, I had received a posting order to report to my Regimental Centre at Dehra Dun. The problem was – how to get there; we could travel in considerable discomfort to Lahore on one of the few trains running and then try and get a place on a troop special going to India. There was little or no animosity towards Europeans, so we would be safe enough but not our heavy baggage or household goods. The railway administration would book our baggage but there was no guarantee that it would arrive intact or at all. Thus it looked that we would either have to leave it behind or lose it en route. Fortune smiled on us and provided a solution which enabled Pauline and I to set forth on an unusual and interesting journey. I had heard that the Indian staff and student Officers, servants, and India's share of the divided Staff College were to be repatriated by a special train, which would run direct from Quetta to Delhi – the destination was later changed to Amballa as Delhi was cut off from the Punjab by floods, but from Amballa it would be possible to travel to Dehra Dun by the ordinary train service. I approached the Commandant and was told that I was mad – to identify myself with Hindu and Sikh Officers on this train would lead to my wife and being attacked and probably murdered. I replied that I did not think this very likely as the train was to have a strong escort, but to travel any other way would invariably mean the loss of my kit. Authority finally washed it hands of us and agreed that we could go at our own risk. In actual fact another British couple and ten British single Officers also came on the special.

I wrote an account of this journey and this was published in the "Railway Gazette" in 1948; with their permission I reproduce it in full:-

"In October 1947, the final course at the Staff College, Quetta closed and there were a number of officers of the Indian Dominion, together with military and civilian staff, to be repatriated from Pakistan to India. As a result a special train was ordered to carry them from Quetta to Amballa, which was

117

selected as the dispersal point from which onward journeys might be made by the ordinary train service.

In view of the amount of baggage, private cars and other equipment to be conveyed, the train was split into two – a baggage train to leave Quetta on October 17 and arrive at Amballa on October 19; and a personnel train to leave on October 18 and arrive on October 20. The route was to be the N.W.R. main line to Samasata via Sibi and Rohri and thence to Amballa via Bhatinda, Dhuri Junction and Rajpura in order to avoid the disturbed area around Lahore. The writer travelled on the personnel special.

The train consisted of 15 bogies and seven four wheelers, carrying approximately 50 commissioned officers, 50 subordinate officers and nearly 1000 civilains, in nearly every case accompagnied by their families. An escort of 170 men (Hindu and Sikh soldiers awaiting repatriation) was provided.

The Make up consisted of:

1 "FSQ"	(first/second composite)
1 "MK"	(military kitchen car)
3 "MS"	(special military cars for officers)
1 "MSLR"	(special military car/luggage and brake composite)
4 "M"	(military cars)
4 "T"	(third class)
1 "TLR"	(third/luggage and brake composite)
5 "C"	(four wheeled goods wagons)
1	parcel van
1	goods brakevan

An elaborate defence system of light machine gun posts was provided – on the engine, on the goods brake in the rear and at stategic points along the train. All the posts were linked to a ten line exchange in the train H.Q.; the wires being laid along the roofs of the carriages.

The approximate timings were as follows :

	1st Part	2nd Part	
Quetta dep	13.00	14.00	Train divided owing to Bolan Pass
Sibi arr	19.30	20.30	incline
dep	22.00		October 18
Rohri arr	06.30		October 19
dep	09.30		
Samasata arr	20.00		
dep	21.00		
Bhatinda arr	09.30		October 20
dep	10.30		
Amballa arr	17.30		

The train actually arrived at 2030 hrs on October 21.

The first part started about 30 mins late behind an "HG" 2–8–0, the standard engine for the Bolan Pass route. On starting the descent of the pass (gradients 1 in 25), the train attempted to run away and was only brought under control with the greatest dificulty. On arrival at the first station, Hirok, examination showed that several of the carriage brakes were defective, in spite of having been passed fit to run by the train examiner at Quetta. As a result the descent was made at at an average speed of 5–10 m.p.h. causing considerable delay to the "Quetta-Karachi Mail" following behind. Sibi was reached at about 9.30 p.m. the second portion arriving 30 mins later.

The whole train then left about 2 hours late behind a "HPS" 4–6–0. This engine proved quite incapable of handling the load, and further delays were caused by leaky vacuum connections and cylinders. Rohri was reached, therefore at 11 a.m. on October 19 or about 5 hours late. A halt of three hours to clean and water the train occurred and we restarted on the main line at 2 p.m. Some trouble occurred owing to the refusal of the Pakistan driver to accept our escort on his engine, as he stated that a Hindu escort would murder him – this was the only driver not to accept an escort. However after the escort was withdrawn to the first

119

vehicle, he started, and did some smart running with his Canadian-built war time "CWC" 2–8–0, and by the evening of October 19 we had gained one hour. What happened after that in the night, the writer does not know, but we woke up on October 20, only eight miles beyond Samasata, although by then we had acquired two "HGs" in lieu of our Canadian engine. As we were now nearing the Pakistan-Indian border defence precautions were redoubled, but luckily no incident occurred.

On this section the drivers seemed to have distinct ideas of their own importance, twice starting without the guard's "all right". On arrival at McCleodganj Road Junction, the last station in Pakistan, the engine came off and proceeded to the rear of the train ready to push us over the border. A special escort of Pakistan (Bahawalpur State) troops relieved our escort on the engine. The station presented a deserted appearance as no ordinary traffic was running, and, in fact, no guard was available to take the train on. An Anglo Indian controller eventually stepped into the breach. A deserted office was labelled "Head Neutral Train Examiner", presumably to deal with traffic between the new Dominions.

On arrival at the next station – Hindumalkote – an ordinary wayside station with a running road and a loop, the engine immediately uncoupled, was attached to a train of wagons standing on the loop and departed for Pakistan.

We were now in India and on the new Eastern Punjab Railway formed to operate that part of the N.W.R. (Delhi and Ferozepore Divisions) located in India. Another long delay occurred (3 hours) while an engine was being sent from Bhatinda, and, as a result, we were still in Bhatinda Yard on the morning of October 21. We left behind an E.P.R. Canadian 2–8–0 to traverse the Sikh States of Nabha, Jind, and Patiala. On this section every station was congested with refugees as no pasenger trains were running on any section of the E.P.R. Shortly after leaving Bhatinda we stopped at a wayside station where the local Sikh villagers had prepared sufficient chappaties (unleavened bread) to feed the whole train, as a gesture towards refugees arriving from Pakistan. Shortly after restarting our engine began to fail

120

and halts had to be made between stations to allow a head of steam to be got up. So long, in fact, did we take to cover the section Bhatinda-Dhuri Junction, that on nearing the latter place the engine without intimation to anyone, suddenly uncoupled and proceeded to the station for water leaving the train standing "in section".

On arrival at Dhuri, a halt of three hours was made to allow the engine crew to clean the fire and get up steam. As a result we had no further engine trouble and arrived at Rajpura Junction only 20 miles from Amballa at 5 p.m. From here delays occurred at every station so we finally arrived at 8.30 p.m. on October 21.

No unpleasant incident occurred during the whole journey, but several unpredicted events did – a first class dog fight, a sweeper's wife gave birth to a son during the second night, and another woman had to be removed to hospital at Nabha for the same reason, and it was during the upheaval caused by this that one of the cases of non co-operation between driver and guard occurred. The train started without an "all right", and in spite of red flags from the guard and stationmaster, signals and shouts from everyone, and the pulling of the communication cord until it broke, the train ran on for about half a mile before finally it was stopped, leaving the O.C. Troops, the Catering Officer, and the Guard behind. The train then had to be backed up to fetch them".

Pauline and I had a very comfortable journey as we were spared having to travel in one of the "MS". The senior Indian Officer, Colonel "Shiv" Verma, had gone to Amballa by air to prepare for our reception, and had told his wife that she and their son were not to travel alone in a coupé, but in a four berth with another couple. She asked us to come with her so we travelled in a four berth compartment in the "FSQ" – four humans and three dogs. The Military Kitchen Car ("MK") was only included in our train as a convenient way of working it back to India, and was not there to feed us. It was in the charge of a very superior British Warrant Officer, who cared nothing for India or Pakistan, Independence or Partition, riot or civil commotion, but merely that he had to be in Amballa by a certain date to take a British

121

battalion to Bombay for embarkation. He was very co-operative and said that, while as Officers, he could not ration us, if we would buy sufficent food for the journey, his cooks would prepare our meals. One of the Indian Officer Instructors was appointed Catering Officer and we clubbed together for him to buy the foodstuffs. He took up his quarters in the "MK" and at the appropriate times we lined up before him to receive our very excellent meals. I may add that there was no shortage of whisky or beer, but water, particularily for the train's lavatories, was often in very short supply.

Willingdon Bridge near Bally, Eastern Railway. The girder span moved into position.

122

A panoramic view of the Dufferin Bridge over the Ganga, as originally constructed looking at the girder from the right bank up-stream side.

123

A view of the blockhouses at the Kashi (Banaras) end of the Dufferin Bridge.

CHAPTER IX

STAYING ON – THE LAST YEARS – 1948–53.

Our "repatriation" train having safely reached Amballa, we were delighted to find that one of the battalions there was the 2/9th Gurkhas. This was a renaming of the 5/9th in which I had served, and it had been augmented by a number of the original 2/9th, who had returned from the Japanese Prison Camps. We were invited to the celebrations for the Hindu festival of Dasehra, and I was happy to meet many old friends. At the end of the celebrations it happened that a 3 tonner was going to Dehra Dun, on which we were able to cadge a lift, but it could not take all our kit; this posed no problem as we could leave the surplus with the 2/9th to be collected later. The horses, grooms and trap arrived in due course; I was lucky that the Airborne Division had a train going direct from Quetta to Dehra Dun, and one of their staff Officers wanted someone to share the expense of a horse box. We remained in Dehra until January 1948, when I was posted as Chief Staff Officer of the Infantry School at Mhow in Central India. We travelled there by the Frontier Mail to Ratlam, to where the School had sent a staff car to await our arrival; our journey was incident free, but once again the move of the horses presented problems. The railways had returned almost to normal after the Partition disturbances as far as passenger traffic was concerned, but special services such as the provision of horse boxes was still difficult. We could not delay our departure until a box had been found, but luckily, I thought of our Regimental Contractor, the Choudhri. I sent for him and asked him to ration the grooms and horses, get a horse box from the railway, load them into it with rations for the journey, and finally book the box to Mhow, with the necessary change of gauge, and finally send me a bill. All he did was to salaam and say "Acchi bat, Sahib" (very good Sir), and they duly arrived.

Mhow was a an engine changing station on the BB & CI's metre gauge Raputana-Malwa line. This was originally a Government project which was later handed over to the BB &

CI; the portion from Indore to the river Nerbadda was the Holkar State Railway owned by the Maharaja Holkar of Indore, but worked by the BB & CI. The line started from Ajmere on the Ahmadabad to Delhi main line and traversed a number of Indian States on its way to Khandwa on the GIP's broad gauge Delhi line. About half way, it crossed the BB & CI's broad gauge main line on the level at Ratlam, where all three daily passenger trains halted for two to three hours so as to connect with either the Frontier Mails or Delhi Expresses. There was a large engine shed at Mhow and the main line motive power was provided by the BESA "H" Class 4–6–0s. The track was lightly laid and the signalling primative, and as a result speeds were low – over four hours for the 80 miles from Mhow to Ratlam. The light track prevented the use of the "YB" Pacifics and the "H" Class were in such a state of decrepitude that my query to the Driver when travelling was not "Right time – Ratlam?" but "Will she make it to Ratlam" to which the Anglo Indian Driver would reply "I hope so, Your Honour".

The line immediately south of Mhow had gradients as severe as 1 in 40, where it descended from the Central India plateau to the valley of the Nerbadda River. To prevent accidents catch points were inserted on the descent. These were different from the spring loaded points, used on an ascending line to derail runaway wagons found in Britain, as the Indian variety, together with a stop signal, were operated by a pointsman. The points were kept in the derail position and the stop signal at danger until the descending train had come to a dead stop and the Driver had signed the pointsman's book, acknowledging that his train had come to halt and uas completely under control; the pointsman then reversed the points and pulled off the signal.

Pauline and I decided to take our month's annual leave in the hill station of Darjeeling, stopping off en route for a few days in Calcutta. We left Mhow on a Khandwa passenger and changed there into an air conditioned coach on the GIP's Calcutta Mail. This left Bombay (V.T) in the evening of the first day, and passed through Khandwa early on the following morning; it reached Allahabad that evening, where the GIP Restaurant Car was detached and the train handed over to the East Indian. I went forward to see the new engine come on, and as I expected for a lightly loaded Mail, it was an "HP"; the driver was an elderly Anglo Indian, who had his son with him as first fireman. The Guard, also an Anglo Indian, came up to report the load and said "Ooh – ould Driver – ould engine but right time Howrah?", to which the Driver replied "Aye, the ould b-----s be best", and we did reach Howrah on time on the following morning.

Partition had played havoc with the B & A Railway – Assam was completely cut off from India, and in many places the line crossed and recrossed the frontier several times in a few miles. On the other hand there had been no trouble in Bengal and through working and ticketing was still in operation. We left Sealdah by the Darjeeling Mail which entered East Pakistan and re-entered India just short of Siliguri. The only noticeable difference was that we were visited by the Indian Customs, who solemnly put paper seals round our cases; these soon came off by reason of poor gum, but no one seemed to mind. We duly arrived at Siliguri next morning where we breakfasted before boarding the narrow gauge Darjeeling-Himalayan train. Most travellers prefered to go by taxi or bus, which was much faster, but I wished to see the D.H., and my wife loyally agreed – in any event it was much less sick making than a taxi ride on a tortuous mountain road.

The Darjeeling Himalayan Railway was a real curiosity even amongst narrow gauge railways. The Darjeeling Himalayan Railway Co Ltd was formed in 1879 to construct a railway from Siliguri on the then metre gauge North Bengal State section of the Eastern Bengal Railway up to the hill station. The moving spirit behind the formation of the Company was the Agent (General Manager) of the Eastern Bengal, Franklin Prestage. The line of 51 miles, on the 2 ft gauge, had to rise from 200 feet above sea level to a summit of just under 7,400 at Ghum before dropping down to Darjeeling at 6,800 feet. The ruling gradient is generally 1 in 25, but there are some sections of 1 in 22 and one short length of 1 in 20. It was completed to Ghum in 1881 and reached Darjeeling four years later. Unlike the Kalka Simla and Zhob

127

Valley lines, the D.H. was constructed with light rails and ballast and used the side of the existing "cart road" wherever possible. At a number of places trains come to a halt in the village street.

A separate associated company was formed in 1914, the Darjeeling Himalayan Extensions Ltd, to construct two further lines from Siliguri. The Kishenganj line ran south westwards for 70 miles into the adjacent province of Bihar, to meet a branch of the metre gauge Bengal & North Western; the Teesta Valley line went into the foothills on easy gradients for 30 miles to a terminus from whence a ropeway took goods up to the town of Kalimpong. The Kishenganj branch was converted to metre gauge, in 1948, together with a part of the Teesta Valley line as part of the Assam Link Project.

The operation of the main line was more like that of a tramway than a railway. The train staff was in use, but with a system of permissive block, which allowed trains to follow each other through a section. Special 0–4–0 saddle tank locomotives were used; the short wheel base was necessitated by some of the curves being as sharp as 60 ft radius. The locomotives had neither sanding gear nor continous brakes – a curious feature on a hill railway. To gain height, use was made of reversing stations and double loops – the line curving round and passing over itself. The principal train was the Mail, up in the morning and down in the afternoon, connecting with the broad gauge Mails at Siliguri. The make up was eight bogies and one or two four wheeled vans. This was hauled by one of the tank engines some seven miles across the flat plain to Sukna where the train was divided. The first portion consisted of a I Class saloon car (pre-war with bar), a II Class, a postal sorting carriage and a brake inter; the III Class portion with the vans followed behind. The train crew numbered ten – the usual three on the footplate (driver and two firemen), together with two boys who sat on the buffer beam with a heap of sand between them, which was put on the rails by hand as required. There was a head brakeman and three assistants (one per coach) and finally the guard; it was usual for the crew other than the guard to be ethnic Gurkhas. Going up hill, the brakemen sat on the roof of the last vehicle, with a rope communication to

128

the engine; down hill a brakeman stood on a platform on the end of each coach, with his head looking over the roof and his foot on the brake lever, which he pressed down when the engine whistled for brakes. The carriages were lit by electricity supplied from the engine's headlight dynamo by means of electric couplers.

Trains often ran in convoys of three – two parts of a Mail or Passenger and one Goods. On arrival at the lower end of a reversing station, which was neither a block post nor staffed, a brakeman would jump off and immediately the train had cleared the points, he threw over the lever and his train immediately backed up the next section. The following trains, meanwhile, had halted nose to tail waiting for the first to get clear. When the first train was clear, its brakeman reversed the points for the second train, and followed it at the double leaping aboard before it had gone very far. This procedure was followed at the upper end when the locomotive once again pulled its train.

The engines were never turned, so to facilitate reverse running, the coal bunkers were forward of the cab and extended over the top of the rear of the boiler. The engines had a very curious appearance – the short coupled wheel base, with outside cylinders, gave a very generous overhang at each end. On top of the boiler between the chimney and the dome was the small saddle tank and behind the dome was situated the coal bunker. Two screw jacks were positioned, one on each running plate and two wooden re-railing levers were carried in a rack one on each side of the boiler – minor derailments were frequent. These locomotives, the "B" Class had lasted nearly the whole life of the railway. The earliest were built by Sharp, Stewart & Co in 1889 with further batches delivered up to 1903. The first of the North British built locomotives were received in 1904, followed by further batches in 1913 and 1914 and three more came from Baldwins in 1917. The final three were built from imported parts at the Company's own Tindharia workshops which cling to the hillside at an altitude of 4,000 feet. The D.H. had two curiosities – a 0–4–0 +0–4–0 Garratt acquired in 1911 and a 2 ft gauge light Pacific, on the Kishenganj extension, the only one of its kind in India.

We returned as we had come by the afternoon Mail, and were the only I Class passengers. The train began to lose time after a while, but this did not worry us as the Broad Gauge Mail had to await our arrival, and I had wired Siliguri for our dinners to be ready. The arrival was, in fact, a few minutes after the departure time of the connecting Mail and on pulling into Siliguri, the Duty ASM was waiting with coolies ready to hurry us into the other train. We were pushed into it and on the point of departure two dinner trays were handed in and we were off – very smart work.

The policy of the Government of India was to leave small and unimportant narrow gauge lines in private ownership, but the D.H. was purchased in 1948 as the road bed of the extensions was required for the Assam Link. Services on the Darjeeling and Teesta Valley lines continued to be operated by the North East Frontier Railway – mixed gauge was laid between Siliguri and the point of divergence of the Link line. This continued until both lines were severely damaged by floods and landslips – the Link was repaired immediately, but the Teesta valley line was never re-opened. There was some talk of doing the same on the Darjeeling line but it was finally decided to re-open it with steam traction as a tourist attraction. Cook's Overseas Timetable for October 1990 shows one up and one down train daily, connecting with the broad gauge Darjeeling Mail to and from Calcutta via the Farakka Dam – each taking about seven hours for the 51 miles. The later broad gauge Assam Link did not go into Siliguri but to New Jalpaiguri, 4 miles to the south; to make a connection, the 2 ft gauge was extended south along the old broad gauge alignment.

The father in law of my GSO II at the School, Mr Sircar an Indian Christian, was the Deputy Chief Commercial Manager of the East Indian. He had been a very senior Officer of the North Western and, as a Christian, saw no reason to leave that Railway. Unforunately, he had a Hindu name and this resulted in threats to his life, so he came over to India, where he was received without enthusiasm for originally opting for Pakistan. This caused him to be appointed to a post below that to which his seniority should have entitled him. His son in law had advised him that we would be passing through Calcutta, so on arrival at Sealdah, we found a car waiting to take us to his house where we could spend the day, before catching the Bombay Mail that evening. He very kindly drove us to Howrah, and as we had some time in hand, we asked him into our air conditioned compartment to have a whisky; the coach attendant was sent to get two sodas from the platform mineral water stall. After a long interval, he returned saying that he could not find the vendor, and should he get the sodas from the train "soda wallah". A compartment in all long distance trains was set aside for a vendor of minerals and ice, but these were more expensive than those purchased from platform stalls. Mr Sircar, smelling a racket, told the attendant to go again and find the missing vendor, but he demurred saying that the departure time was now near. Mr Sircar angrily replied, saying "I am your new Deputy Chief Commercial Manager, and this train will not leave until the platform vendor is found". Meanwhile the starting signal came off, and the engine began whistling for the "all right". The Guard then arrived, carrying his lantern showing a red light to the engine, and asking with some asperity to whom should he book the delay. He got the same answer. By now we had given up all hope of having a whisky and only wanted the train to depart. However, after about five minutes, the attendant returned with the vendor and two sodas – we quickly paid for them – Mr Sircar, having made his point, detrained – the guard reversed his lantern to green – the engine whistled – and we were off – ten minutes delay duly booked to the Deputy Chief Commercial Manager.

We had to change into the metre gauge train at Khandwa about 4 am, and should we have missed this connection we should have had to hang about until the next train at about noon. Unfortunately, the Mail, which had been keeping time, was delayed just before Khandwa by a goods train failing in section. We ran into Khandwa at the exact departure time of the Mhow train – leaving Pauline to bring over the coolies with our baggage, I shot over to the metre gauge platform and there was the train with the starting signal off. Not seeing the Guard anywhere I hurried to the engine, and luckily the Driver was one Walter

Mack of Mhow shed, who in his spare time was the leader of a four piece dance band, which played at the Mhow Club on Saturdays. I said half in jest – "Dont you dare start that engine, Walter Mack, until my wife gets over or you will never play at the Club again". He replied cheerfully "Certainly not, Sir". Meanwhile the Guard came up and we were safely installed in our compartment, but the train did not start. After a while there was a knock on the door and there was the Guard, saying – "any service for me, Sir,(Indian English for "is there anything further you want") or may I start train now?.

The period covered by this Chapter, the first five years of Independence. saw a number of changes on Indian Railways. Most of the pre-war amenities were restored and time keeping was generally good, at least as far as Mail and Express trains were concerned. There had been a large influx of Canadian and American locomotives and the Indian Railways had designed two broad gauge classes based on them – the WP streamlined Pacific for passenger work and the WG 2–8–2 for goods trains. The new locomotive works at Chittaranjan were now in operation and beginning to turn out Indian built engines. Staff morale had been restored by two Commissions, one dealing with pay and one dealing with working conditions – the former considerably increased the pay scales for all grades. The Anglo Indian staff had been very worried about their position after Independence – would their loyalty to the old British Government cost them their jobs, if nothing worse. The Prime minister, Pandit Nehru, realising how much the railways depended on the community, not only left them in their jobs but continued their privileges for ten years. These privileges were such things as reserved job vacancies, their special schools with English as their "regional language" and so on.

Two major engineering works were carried out in this period – the first was the "rescue" of the Assam Railway by the construction of the "Assam Link". The new frontier had completely isolated the metre gauge lines in Assam and the contiguous part of north Bengal. The new line started at Kishenganj on the Bengal & North Western and used the D.H.

alignment through Siliguri to the Teesta River; after crossing it, it ran eastwards in the narrow corridor between the Pakistan frontier and the mountains using short sections of the B & A and Bengal Dooars Railways before joining the old East Bengal north bank line just inside Assam. The total length of 143 miles, which had to cross three major rivers, was opened in December 1949. The second was the reconstruction of the G.I.P's ghat lines to Poona and Igatapuri; these had been built to a very tight loading gauge so that the tunnels would not accept standard broad gauge rolling stock. Over a period of two years, without interupting traffic, the tunnels were opened out or new lines laid.

Passenger trains remained much as they had been pre-war, not very frequent or very fast but a new service, the "Janata" Expresses, was introduced between major cities – these were III Class only trains running with the same stops and speeds as Mail trains. An effort was made to reduce the number of passenger classes by withdrawing lying down accomodation from II Class with the idea of the abolition in the future of the Intermediate class, but this proved so unpopular that it was soon restored – reorganisation of the different classes would have to wait for a decade or so longer.

All broad gauge and many metre gauge lines were already owned and operated by the Government at the time of Independence; the only railways of any size remaining in other hands were those owned by Indian Native States. They ceased to be independent at the end of 1949, when the Rulers lost their ruling powers, and for the time their railways were taken over by the adjacent State railway – the GIP took over the Nizam's State, the BB & CI the Jodhpur, Bikanir State, Jaipur State and other lines in Gujerat and Kathiawar and the South Indian the Mysore Railway. This cleared the way for a major reorganisation, the first phase of which was completed in 1952. A number of changes were made in the succeeding years and the final form which exists today was:

The Western Railway – based on Bombay.
Broad Gauge – BB & CI

Metre Gauge – BB & CI, (less Rewari-Delhi and Rewari-Bhatinda sections), Jaipur State, Mewar State and railays in Guijerat and Kathiawar.

The Northern Railway – based on Delhi.
Broad Gauge – Eastern Punjab Railway (that part of the NWR still in India), East Indian west of Mughal Serai.
Metre Gauge – Rewari-Delhi and Rewari-Bhatinda sections of the old BB&CI, Jodhpur and Bikanir State Railways.

The Central Railway – based on Bombay.
Broad Gauge – GIP less Dhond-Raichur section.

The Eastern Railway – based on Calcutta.
Broad Gauge – East Indian east of Mughal Serai, Calcutta suburban from Sealdah.

The South Eastern Railway – based on Calcutta
Broad Gauge – the greater part of the Bengal Nagpur.

The South Central Railway – based on Secunderabad.
Broad Gauge – Nizam's State, parts of GIP, M & SM, and Bengal Nagpur.
Metre Gauge – Nizam's State, part of M & SM.

The Southern Railway – based on Madras.
Broad Gauge and Metre Gauge – South Indian, Mysore Railway and part of M & SM.

The North Eastern Railway – based on Gorakhpur.
Metre Gauge – Oudh & Tirhut (old Bengal & North Western and Rohillakund & Kumaon Railways).

The North Eastern Frontier Railway. – based on Gauhati.
Broad Gauge – BG Assam Link
Metre Gauge – MG Assam Link, parts of Bengal and Assam (old Eastern Bengal and Assam Bengal Railways), within the old province of Assam

134

It was unfortunate that, just as the Railways were returning to normal, there occured a spate of attacks on and robberies of passengers in running trains. The thieves took advantage of the state of the door and window fastenings of the Upper Class carriages, neglected during the war. The attacks were mainly confined to those trains or through carriages on purely overnight journeys – the Delhi-Dehra Dun Express and the Delhi-Amritsar and Delhi-Kalka through carriages were in this category. The thief would observe whether any of the I Class compartments were in single occupancy and whether the occupant was worth robbing or likely to put up a strong resistance – Ladies travelling alone were a particular target. He would hide on top of the battery box underneath the carriage, and in due course get onto the running board, force the door or window, and after having stabbed and robbed the passenger, jump off the train when it next slowed down. The mother in law of a British Officer serving at the Indian Signal School was one such sad case. She was attacked between Delhi and Saharanpur, but might have survived had she had received prompt medical attention on arrival but, unfortunately, a typical Indian argument arose as to whether she should be taken to the Railway or Civil Hospital – should she be taken in a taxi or a tonga and more important, who would pay for it – by the time a decision was reached, she had died. The Government took strong measures by raising a special Police Force under a Deputy Inspector General, but more important, by having the doors and windows fitted with new tumbler bolts.

Pauline and I had an disconcerting experience when travelling on the Frontier Mail from Ratlam to Bombay – a youth under the seat of our compartment. The Conductor, on the train's arrival at Ratlam, found that he could not open the door of our compartment with his key, as it appeared to be fastened on the inside; he then sent a coolie round to other side to get in and unbolt it. We entrained assuming that the compartment had been checked for intruders. The train started and just as we were getting into bed Pauline said – "I suppose that there is no one under the seat". I, of course, laughed at this but said that I would make a check, starting with the bathroom, when a yell came from

135

Pauline "there is someone under the seat". Most unusually, as I normally did not travel armed, I had my automatic pistol with me, so covering the intruder, I ordered him to come out, while Pauline pulled the communication cord and the train came to a stop. The problem was what to do next. It was the monsoon season and raining hard – looking out I could see the guard coming forward with a lantern and the fireman coming back with a flaming torch, each checking the indicators to find out where the cord had been pulled. I got out and fell into a monsoon ditch with water up to my knees, meanwhile Pauline was covering the intruder with my pistol. A very young Anglo Indian Ticket Inspector then looked out of another compartment, and I told him as a railway official to get down and collect the boy, but got the reply – "ooh, Sir, I am frightened of firearms". Luckily the fireman was made of sterner stuff, so he collected the boy, tied his hands with his own pagree, and pushed him into the servants' compartment to be handed over to the railway police at the next stop. I was of the opinion that the lad was only getting a free ride as the area through which the Frontier Mail ran had no history of robberies and was considered so peaceful that the train did not have the usual armed police escort, and further, it was unlikely that he would have entered the compartment on the off chance that some hours later it would be occupied.

We did a great deal of travelling during these five years; I had to visit Army HQ at Delhi fairly frequently, and Pauline and I made several visits to Bombay and another one to Calcutta. I also took her on ten days leave to Simla; coming back we were lucky to get the two places beside the Driver on the front seat of the railcar so we could enjoy the superb views. Most of my journeys were very comfortable as I became known to the Conductors on The Frontier Mail and was always assured of good service.

Two journeys were especially memorable – the first was a return from Poona during the monsoon; I came down to Bombay by the morning Deccan Queen; it was raining hard and after Kalyan, there appeared to be very little dry land visible. As the Frontier Mail did not leave Bombay until six in the evening, I took a room at the Taj Mahal Hotel, where I would lunch and

136

have a siesta, but on buying a paper, I read that the BB & CI's coast line was flooded and there were serious delays to traffic. This was not unusual – I had caught the Mail of the day before at Ratlam on the odd occasion during the monsoon, but I did want to know if the Mail would run that night. I got through to Bombay Central Station by telephone to learn that the line was open for single line working, but the morning's up Mail would not arrive until between seven and eight that evening and as this formed the rake for the evening down Mail, it was unlikely that this train would leave before ten. We got off about that time and when we had left Bombay Island it seemed as if we were going out to sea, as the line was under water and it was an eerie experience as we splashed our way onward with permanent way men standing at intervals with lanterns waving us on. The second journey was to Delhi, during June, when day temperatures were about 115°F. I had had to postpone my journey owing to a fractured wrist. It was still painful and when I arrived at Ratlam, I heard that the Mail was three hours late, which added to my misery. I had been hoping for an air conditioned compartment, but the Conductor could only give me an ordinary coupé. The blow then fell – he explained that, while he had plenty of ice, all the containers were in use as the train was unusually full because of a party of film personalties travelling to a première at Delhi; he would send a wire, however, to the next station for a container. Arriving there – no container, so the Conductor suggested that an ice block be placed on a sack on the floor. This was done and it certainly cooled the compartment, but the melting ice caused rivulets across the floor to the doors. Sometime in the evening, I got out at a stop with a low platform and in getting back my foot slipped on the wet footboard and I came down heavily on my side; at first I thought that I had broken a rib, the pain was so intense. A memorable journey indeed!.

The Government of India, in 1951 gave us the equivalent of one return air and one return sea passage to be used for a leave ex India. I was now in my fourth year of service with the new Government and it then seemed unlikely that I would be given a fifth. To have gone home, returned, and then to have gone home again permanently at the end of the year, seemed pointless, so we thought we would spend our leave in the Lebanon, at that time a very popular holiday resort. Thomas Cook's Bombay Office made out our itinerary and arranged our tickets and reservations – the B.I. weekly mail boat from Bombay to Basra – air conditioned compartment on the metre gauge Basra-Baghdad Mail – W.L. sleeper on the Taurus Express to Aleppo and finally the D.H.P. railcar to Beirut. Cooks also obtained our Iraq, Turkish, Syrian and Lebanese Visas; there was a slight hiccup over the Syrian Visa as the Consul queried the validity of our joint Passport. This was a "British India – Indian Empire" document issued by the Regional Commissioner for Central India States, in September 1948, in which I was described as a "British Subject by birth" and my occupation as an "Indian Army Officer". Cooks advised me that I should go and see him personally and explain that such Passports were still valid and there were British subjects still serving in the Indian Army. I satisfied him and then asked if he thought I would have the same trouble with the Lebanese Visa. He waved his hands and said "Oh no, the Consul General is on leave and I am in charge of his Consulate, I will merely telephone his Secretary and instruct him to issue the Visa". He was as good as his word and the Visa was duly issued signed "P le Consul Général – R.D.Patel, "SECRETAIRE". This journey practically filled our Passport – seven Visas, as we had to obtain fresh ones for our return journey – three exit permits and our Passport stamped fourteen times at the various frontiers.

We had a very comfortable journey out but I nearly ruined it – remembering my journey to Beirut in 1941, we detrained at Tripoli and looked in the station forecourt for the connecting bus. It was lucky that we were told, in time to get back, that the bus was no more as the railcar continued right up to Beirut. We came back the by same route and joined the Taurus in the evening at Aleppo; I was worried when I noticed that the Wagon Restaurant was not coupled next to our Wagon Lit, but I was reassured when I saw it moving majestically behind a long string of goods wagons. By breakfast time on the next morning we were in Turkey and the

138

W.R. was in its proper place again. We soon learned what had happened – the coupling at the rear had been broken by rough shunting at Beirut so nothing could be put on behind it; what was unfortunate that, unlike the Turkish railways and the L.S.B., the Iraq Railways were going to refuse to accept it at Tel Kotchek. The Chief Steward, however agreed to give us an early dinner before reaching that place, and the W.L. Attendant would be able to give us coffee and rolls from his pantry before reaching Baghdad the next morning. We continued onwards to Basra to in order to board the B.I. Steamer, the Dara, the same ship as on our outward trip and commanded by a delightful character nicknamed "Two Gin Johnston". He was so called as he used to invite first class passengers to his cabin for a pre lunch gin. As soon as he had consumed two, he would announce "now I am going to lunch", whether his guests were ready or not.

It so happened that I was offered another year meaning retirement at the end of 1952, when the Government would have paid for two first class P & O passages; I think the success of out Beirut trip caused us to think of another way home – by train from Basra to London.

Indian built 'WP' class Pacific locomotive.   *Author's Collection*

Author's Collection

Darjeeling-Himalayas Railway – The famous double loop.

DHR 'B' class locomotive. *Author's Collection*

First part of the Darjeeling Mail. Note:- boys sitting on front of engine for hand sanding of track. *Author's Collection*

Second part of Darjeeling Mail at reversing station. *Author's Collection*

FINALE

THE LAST JOURNEY

I heard in 1952 that this would be my last year and that I should finish my service on or shortly after the 31th December; the Government would then grant me one year's leave pending retirement, give my wife and I first class P & O passages, together with a generous baggage allowance. The thought came to us that if we managed to commute the sea passage for cash, we might go home in a more interesting and leisurely fashion, which would allow us to see such places as Istanbul, Athens and Venice and also miss some of England's winter weather.

There were a number of factors in our favour – the first was sterling; at this time the British holiday allowance was only £50 per person. We, however, came under Indian rules and India was awash with sterling as Britain had re-paid the so called "sterling balances"; that was the monies expended by India during the war on behalf of Britain. I see from my old passport that we were allowed £300 each over and above the transportation costs. We intended to travel comfortably, if not in luxury, staying at the best hotels and travelling in sleeping cars – second, that Continental railways still had three classes which helped us greatly. The standard Wagon Lit two berth compartment, now first class, was at this time first class only when in single occupancy; when occupied by two persons, the identical compartment required only a second class rail ticket. Thus, for the rail portion of our journey we only paid first class fares for the portions Basra-Baghdad and Dover-London.

I took a trip to Bombay and interviewed Cooks, who introduced me to a I.I.T., an "Inclusive Independent Tour", now regrettably overtaken by the package tour; this would include rail tickets, sleeper tickets, meal vouchers for train meals, hotel accomodation, transfers to and from stations and finally excursions at Istanbul, Athens and Venice. The whole tour would be worked out in London and would start at Basra, although Cook's Bombay Office would book our steamer passages to

143

Basra. The only arrangements not covered were meals between Baghdad and the Turkish frontier at Islahiye when there was no Restaurant Car, and, in Yugoslavia, whose authorities did not accept Cook's Vouchers.

The planning had not gone very far, when it became obvious that, all being well, there would be a third passenger, a four months old baby. There was much heart searching as neither Pauline nor I wished to abandon a trip that we might never do again. Three things turned the scale – first, my wife hoped to be able to feed the baby herself – second, except for the last short journey from Dover to London, we should have a reserved cabin or compartment the whole way – third, we would not have to carry any of our luggage, as at each point, we should be met by Cook's representative who would deal with it. So we decided on the great adventure.

It so happened that a great friend of ours at the Infantry School, Colonel Mani Badshah, had been posted to the Indian High Commission at Karachi, and he and his wife suggested that we get off the Gulf steamer there, stay with them and continue onward by the next steamer a week later. I was a little worried about my position, as relations between India and Pakistan were lukewarm, so I wrote a tactful letter to the Indian Director of Military Intelligence, stating that, while as a British Officer I could go where I liked on retirement, my wife and I would not go to Karachi if this would cause any embarrassment, adding that we would be staying in the Indian High Commission. Army Headquarters duly agreed.

We left Mhow by the evening train to Khandwa and changed into the Punjab Mail for Bombay arriving there at noon. The Military Forwarding Organisation had sent a representative to take over our heavy baggage, which would be shipped direct to England. One of the tasks which had to be done before we left was to obtain baggage permits from the Customs; as far our heavy stuff going to Britain was concerned, this was a formality, but some bother arose over Pauline's jewellery, all of which she was taking with her as she did want to send it in our heavy luggage. Only what was actually worn was allowed to be taken to Pakistan,

144

and we were told officially that she could not take her jewel case. We explained our predicament to an elderly Anglo Indian Inspector, who merely said "dont declare it" and issued us with our permits.

The Embarkation Commandant had very kindly given our two servants, the bearer and ayah (nursemaid), dock permits to enable them to see us off and we parted with great regrets. Two nights on the steamer and we were in Karachi, where Mani Badshah was waiting to greet us. Mani, although a Hindu, was originally a native of Lahore and with a large and luxuriant moustache looked like a Moslem, and further he had diplomatic status. He had the Pakistan Customs and Immigration Officers falling over themselves to pass us through – "yes, Colonel Badshah, of course, Mrs Mains may go straight through to your car" and "Of course, Colonel Badshah, we should not think of opening Colonel Mains' cases" were some of the remarks that we heard.

We spent an enjoyable week in Karachi in a whirl of diplomatic parties and excursions to the beach at Clifton; daughter Jane, I am afraid, was horribly spoilt and enjoyed every minute. At the end of our stay we embarked on the S.S. *Dwarka* for the sail up the Gulf to Basra. During the voyage we were witnesses to a so called diplomatic incident involving the the Persian authorities at Bushire. The B.I steamers anchor in an open roadstead and passengers and cargo are transferred in local bunder boats. While we were at anchor, the wind and sea got up and the boatmen wished to cast off for home, but one of them alleged that he had been hit by the Dwarka's Chief Officer. The Persian Head of the Customs and the Captain of the Port wished to pursue the matter, and ordered the skipper not to sail without permission and one of the bunder boats to remain to take them off. The wind and the sea continued to rise and the bunder boat soon cast off and headed for shore. Our Captain refused to wait any longer on a lee shore so he upped anchor and set sail. The two Persians, initially furious, soon settled down to a pleasant sail to Kermanshah, travelling first class at the Company's expense. We were much amused later to read in a copy of the "Times" of Persia's

145

diplomatic protest, alleging kidnapping and ill treatment of the two Officers.

We arrived at Basra and booked in at the Shatt al Arab Hotel where we were handed a very bulky envelope from Cook's Basra Office; this contained out tickets, reservations, hotel and meal vouchers, together with a printed itinerary. (I still have this and it is reproduced as an Appendix.) The next evening we set off for Baghdad in an air conditioned two berth sleeper; as this was on the metre gauge, it was somewhat of a tight fit for the two of us and Jane. There was no necessity on this occasion to stay a night in Baghdad, but we had booked a room at the Zia Hotel to rest in during the day. That evening we said farewell to Michael Zia and Jesus, his barman, whom I had known since my time in Baghdad in 1941. We often wondered what became of them after the murder of the King and his Prime Minister, Nuri Pasha; they were Chaldaen Christians and Michael was a staunch supporter of Nuri.

The Taurus Express, which still left in the evening, had one notable alteratiom – the W.L. Restaurant Car no longer penetrated into Syria or Iraq, but was detached at Islahiye on the Turkish frontier which we would not reach until the evening of the third day. The Sleeping Car Attendant, however, told us that we could get breakfast next morning at the Mosul station restaurant and also on the following morning at Aleppo – he would provide snacks and drinks for the other meals from his pantry. We very fortunate that our compartment was the one at the end next to the pantry, as it had a separate washroom. (see Chapter IV). This became Jane's room, where she slept comfortably in her Carrycot. One of the problems on the journey was that most of the countries traversed had galloping inflation and had introduced very strict rules regarding the import and export of currency and valubles and the encashment of travellers cheques. The first impact was at Nusaybin, where the Customs wished to list all our valubles to enable us to take them out when we left Turkey. The travellers cheques posed no problems but my wife's jewellery did – the listing of all the items onto the official form would have taken a long time, even if described in English,

146

but was quite impossible in Turkish. After a while the Customs Officer had a bright idea – to seal the jewel case. It was duly wrapped in a silk handkerchief, tied across both ways with string and the official lead seals applied. Shades of the Indian Customs' paper seals – the string could be easily taken off and replaced without disturbing the seals.

We finally crossed into Turkey at 5 pm at Islahiye on the third day and there in a siding with its kitchen chimney quietly smoking was our Restaurant Car. I had noticed that the Vouchers for our meals had a detachable portion, which was for a reserved seat; shortly after the Car had been attached I went to enquire about the time of dinner – I was amazed that the Chef de Brigade produced the duplicate copy of our seat voucher and enquired if this was for me. To find that this document had penetrated from Berkeley Street to the wilds of Turkey showed a very high degree of organisation, but that was to be expected of the Cooks of those days. The fourth day found us up on the cheerless Anatolian plateau, but towards evening we neared Ankara and the double line and bright lights of suburban stations. A stop at Ankara after dinner and on to reach Hydar Pasha after breakfast on the fifth day.

It had been a comfortable journey and not without interest on the railway scene – once again the Taurus was a mixed train in Iraq and Syria hauled by antique locomotives, but an Express in Turkey where the motive power was enormous German built 2–10–0s or 2–10–2s. The schedule was the same as it had been in 1951 and indeed in 1941, the main difference being that the Taurus now kept time. The track, except in the vicinity of Ankara and Hyder Pasha, was single and the signalling rudimentary. We found that, except in the vicinity of a few major towns or stations, a complete absense of fixed signals from Tel Kotchek to Hydar Pasha and from Athens to Belgrade. Trains were operated on a telegraphic crossing order system and stations had a warning target in advance of the facing points with a pointsman sitting on the point lever showing a green flag or lamp.

Cooks representative was waiting at Hydar Pasha with a car to take us to our Hotel, the Park, situated just below Taksim Square with a glorious view from our room over the Bosphorus. Once again I was caught up in the maze of financial regulations and unwittingly breached them, which could have had serious consequences. I had cashed a travellers cheque in the Restaurant Car and received 8 Turkish Lira to the £1. This was quite in order and was at the official rate of exchange. During the ride to our Hotel, our courier said that he would get us 12 Lira to the £1, which I accepted. Later the Hotel barman offered 13, but I had already made my arrangements. It did not dawn on me until later that this was highly illegal, and had the outgoing Customs counted my Travellers Cheques against the Currency Form from Nusaybin and found some missing with no Bank Invoices to show where they had been cashed, I might have been in trouble. I need not have worried, however, as when we came to embark on the Barletta, our courier, merely had a word or two with a Customs Officer and were were taken straight on board, neither our Currency Form nor Pauline's jewel case was looked at. I suppose that the Courier and the Customs Officer split my tip. We travelled in Europe in the subsequent ten or twenty years and found that whenever we had the services of a Cook's Courier, we went straight through the Police and Customs without either ourselves or our baggage being looked at.

We had wished to travel direct by rail from Istanbul, but the Iron Curtain had descended on Bulgaria, and travel from Istanbul via Thessaloniki was not comfortable as there was no Sleeping Car service. There was a very comfortable steamer service to the Piraeus, provided by the Italian Adriatica Line and this had the advantage of bringing Athens into our itinerary. The ship, the Barletta of 1900 tons, was like a large yacht with superb food and very few passengers. There must have been a change in her sailing times; our itinerary gave our departure at midnight and arrival at the Piraeus at 7 am on the third day, but I remenber that we embarked before lunch and were due in after lunch on the next day. We actually arrived at about noon, much to our annoyance as we had hoped to lunch on board.

We put up at the Grande Bretagne, where I had stayed on an Imperial Airways overnight stop before the war. Greece was in

148

the throes of severe inflation; in fact, when you saw the price of some article given as "5 drachma", it did not mean that at all but 5,000, people no longer bothered to show the noughts. This time I had got the hang of currency restrictions, and by the time we left, I had a number of bank invoices showing that I had cashed my Travellers Cheques at the official rate. Our Courier warned us of possible difficulties in paying for meals in Yugoslavia – the Restaurant Car would not take Travellers Cheques nor drachmas, and it was not possible to obtain Yugoslav dinars in Greece. He said that they would take English money, but I did not think that I had enough. A very long and tedious visit to a Bank, accompagnied by the filling in of many forms, enabled me to cash a £2 cheque and then have this paid as £2 in English notes with the whole transaction being recorded in my Passport. Cooks could obtain neither Greek nor Yugoslav rail tickets in London, so we had to obtain these from Cook's local office for the journey from Athens to the Italian frontier; sleeper tickets, and meal vouchers for use in Greece, we already had as these were for use in Wagon Lits vehicles.

The Larissa Station in Athens was one of those annoying ones where passengers were kept penned in a waiting room until shortly before departure, so I had little opportunity to examine our locomotive – it was probably a Skoda built oil burning 2–10–0. It was a good thing that I did not hang about on the platform as without warning we set off with a tremendous jolt and our sleeping car attendent had to scramble aboard.

We left Athens at 11.35 am on the first day, reached Thessalonika that evening, Skopje the next morning, Belgrade that second evening, and arrived at Venice at 4.45 pm on the third day. Lunch and dinner on the first day was in the W.L. Restaurant Car for which we had vouchers. This car came off at Thessalonika and the Yugoslav Car was attached at Skopje in time for breakfast. We need not have worried about money as when the Chief Steward came round he had a tray containing most of the currencies of Western Europe, including drachmas.

Our train was the post war Simplon Orient, the successor to the pre war "de Luxe" Simplon Orient Express but now no longer a

"Grand Express". It was somewhat of a hotch potch – from Athens, it comprised sleeping cars and through coaches for Paris and Munich, togther with the WL Restaurant Car and Greek coaches to be detached at Thessaloniki; the Yugoslav Restaurant Car was from Skopje to Belgrade and carriages from Sofia were added at Nish. The Belgrade stop lasted for over an hour as the Paris and Munich portions had to be re-marshalled into two separate trains. The rift between "east" and "west" was reflected in the running of our train – no longer did the WL Sleeping Car attendent go the whole way from Athens to Paris, a Greek was replaced by a Yugoslav at the frontier and the latter was replaced again at the Italian border. Although the Greek and Yugoslav wore the traditional WL chocolate coloured uniform, the service, although adequate, was inferior to that we experienced from Italy onwards. The Sleeping Car itself was of Class "Y" with eleven compartments, each with its wash basin within the compartment; they were the most numerous class running in Europe and some dated from 1930; they were the last Cars to be built with the traditional dogleg partition between pairs of compartments. The train was constantly being remarshalled as only the through Paris and Munich coaches crossed the frontier, the Greeks and Yugoslavs providing sectional carriages for local traffic. The scenery in Greece was superb as the line hugs the coast and crosses innumerable ravines by spectacular bridges, but on the second morning, in southern Yugoslavia, it seemed that we were back in Anatolia, a featureless plain with small villages each with its mosque. The third morning found us in Slovenia where the scenery and villages were identical to those in Austria.

We spent a very enjoyable ten days in Venice, although Pauline was beginning to find carrying Jane somewhat tiring, when we were sightseeing on foot. Near the end of our stay, we had two days of fog as thick as an old London "pea souper", when all traffic on the canals and lagoons came to a halt. This co-incided with Pauline catching a cold and having to stay in; further she found that she could no longer feed Jane, so I went out and bought tins of "Carnation" milk, which seemed to do the trick. The onward journey by sleeper to Calais and the Golden

150

Arrow Pullman to Victoria calls for no comment and we arrived there at 6.30 pm on 26th February, having left Bombay on the 9th of January. Our stopovers were four days at Istanbul, a week each at Karachi and Athens and ten days at Venice.

It is interesting to compare our journey with the timings and facilities available later; twenty years on in 1973 the journey was still feasible and quicker – the B.I. Gulf service was still running but only twice a month instead of weekly, and there had been no change in the Basra Mail. The Taurus had been considerably accelerated, and the Turks had constructed a new direct line, within Turkey, by passing Aleppo; this ran via Gaziantep and joined the original Berlin-Bagdad Bahn at Karkamis, where it crossed the Euphrates. The Baghdad Sleeping Car ran once weekly via Aleppo and once weekly via Gaziantep, with the Restaurant Car between Gaziantep and Hydar Pasha only. It still left in the evening but arrived at Hydar Pasha in the evening of the fourth day, an acceleration of about twelve hours. The Simplon Orient had been reconstituted as four trains – the Direct Orient, Paris-Belgrade, and the Tauern Orient, Munich-Belgrade, with through sleeping cars and carriages to Athens and Istanbul. There was still a general post at Belgrade, from where the Athens and Istanbul portions were taken on by the Athens and Marmora Expresses. Restaurant cars were still provided over most of the route, and the Athens to Paris run had been accelerated by about twelve hours.

To day, even before the Gulf War, such a journey would be well nigh impossible and not very comfortable. The B.I. Gulf service is no more and the Taurus goes no further than Gaziantep or Aleppo. The Direct Orient has been taken off and there is no longer a direct service to Paris. It would be possible to travel from Athens to Venice on the Venezia Express, with a U.S.S.R. or Hungarian Sleeping Car to Belgrade and a Yugoslav one thence to Venice, where, after an eight hour wait, the Rialto Express would continue to Paris.

Now a days there is little or no first class or sleeper traffic over long distances as those with money go by air. Most of the long distance trains now carry second class couchettes and light refreshments trolleys rather than Restaurant Cars. We went when long distance rail travel, although not so luxurious as pre war, was still comfortable.

Taurus Express crossing the Duck' Bill in the 1950's through Hyder Pasha-Baghdad sleeping car third vehicle. *John Price*

Hyder Pasha Station. *John Price*

152

Simplon Orient Express Dining Car coupled to 'Y' class sleeping car.

John Price

Simplon Orient Express Dining Car at Piraeus.

John Price

Appendix A

COOK/WAGON-LITS INCLUSIVE INDEPENDENT TOUR
No 11126/BH for Lt Col & Mrs A.A. MAINS

(Page 1.)

HOTEL SHATT-AL-ARAB Class of travel FIRST

Sat 24 Jan 1953
BASRA – arrive by B.I.S.N. Steamer S.S. Dwarka.
Thos Cook & Son's inclusive arrangements commence with provision of Hotel accomodation at Basra. Cost of transfers at Basra are not included and are to be arranged locally.
Sun 25
Sleeping Car berths from Basra to Baghdad have been applied for, if reserved, the ticket will be sent to you at the Shatt-al-Arab Hotel, Please emquire for our letter.
BASRA (Ma'gil)dep 1830
Coupons are provided for dinner, early morning tea, and breakfast on the train.
(For BAGHDAD)
....

(Page 2)

HOTEL ZIA Class of Travel SECOND

Mon 26 (From BASRA)
BAGHDAD (West) arr 0915
Transfer on arrival – See Note "J"
Transfer on departure – See Note "K"
Berths in Sleeping Car reserved. Tickets with Hotel Vouchers,
BAGHDAD (West) dep 20.30
Tue 27 to Thu 29 EN ROUTE
Meals en route between Baghdad and Islahiye (Dep 16.55 Wed Jan 28) may be obtained on the train, cost refundable.
Dinner in Restaurant Car (Wed Jan 28)
Plain breakfast, luncheon and dinner in Restaurant Car (Thurs Jan 29)
(For HYDAR PASHA)
....

(Page 3)

HOTEL PARK Class of travel SECOND/FIRST steamer
Fri 30 JANUARY (From BAGHDAD)
Plain breakfast in Restaurant Car.
Transfer on arrival – See Note "J"
Excursion "B" (Schedule attached)
Sat 31 to Mon 2 FEBRUARY.
Sat Jan 31 Excursion "A" (Schedule attached)
Please make an early call at our Istanbul Office to ascertain embarkation
particulars of S.S Barletta.

Please exchange Voucher at our Istanbul Office for steamer tickets
Istanbul – Piraeus.
Tue 3
Transfer on departure – See Note "K"
Cabin No 12 reserved on S.S.Barletta, Istanbul to Piraeus (Food
included)
ISTANBUL dep 2400
(By S.S. BARLETTA)
Wed 4
AT SEA
(For PIRAEUS)
....
(Page 4)

HOTEL GRANDE BRETAGNE Class of travel SECOND
(From ISTANBUL)
Tue 5 FEBRUARY
PIRAEUS arr 0700
Fri 6 to Wed 11
IN ATHENS
Fri 6 Feb Excursion "B" (Schedule atached)
Please exchange voucher at our Athens Office for second class rail tickets
Athens to Trieste.
Thu 12
Transfer on departure – See Note "K"
Berths in Sleeping Car Athens to Venice reserved, tickets with Hotel
Vouchers

155

ATHENS dep 1135
Luncheon and dinner in Restaurant Car.
Fri 13
En route through Yugoslavia
Meals between Thessalonika and Venice can be obtained on the train,
cost refundable.
Idomeni (Greek Customs) arr 0143
dep 0205
Gevgeli (Yugoslav Customs)arr 0310
dep 0425
....

(Page 5)

HOTEL EUROPA BRITANNIA Class of Travel SECOND

Sat 14 FEBRUARY (From ATHENS)
Sezana (Yugoslav Customs) arr 1151
dep 1241
Poggioreale Campagna (Italian Customs) arr 1250
dep 1310
VENICE (Santa Lucia)arr 1645
Gondola to Hotel
Sun 15 to Tue 24

IN VENICE
Accomodation in Venice is based on en pension terms, and no refund can
be made for meals not taken.
Sunday 15 Feb Excursions "A" & "B" (Schedule attached)
Wed 25
Gondola to station
Berths in Sleeping Car Venice to Calais reserved, tickets with Hotel
Vouchers
VENICE (Santa Lucia) dep 1705
Dinner in Restaurant Car
Domodossola (Italian Customs)arr 2342
dep 0005
....

(Page 6)

156

Class of travel SECOND/FIRST
Thu 26
BRIGUE (Swiss Customs)arr 0048
dep 0055
VALLORBE (Swiss/French Customs)arr 0324
dep 0348
Plain breakfast in Reataurant Car
PARIS (Lyon)arr 0916
Transfer across Paris from Lyon station to Nord station will be
arranged by our Representative to whom please apply.
Pullman car seats from Paris to Calais and Dover to London applied for,
if reserved, tickets will be handed to you in exchange for enclosed voucher
by our Representative arranging your transfer.

PARIS (Nord)dep 1230
Luncheon in Pullman Car
CALAIS (Maritime)arr 1544
dep 1605
DOVER (Marine)arr 1623
dep 1658
LONDON (Victoria)arr 1830
Thos Cook & Son's inclusive arrangements terminate on arrival London.
....

(Author's Note: On arrival at Venice, we found that the 1705 Paris train
had a through Sleeping Car to Calais, worked round the Ceinture Railway
from the Lyon station to the Nord station and attached to the 1230 train
for Calais. As this would cut out changing trains and stations in Paris,
we had our reservations altered.)

NOTES "J" & "K"

Cooks arranged our transfers in private cars or taxis.

EXCURSIONS

Istanbul

"A" – by private car in morning to St Sophia – Sultanahmet Mosque – Hippodrome – Square of Beyazit – Suleiman Mosque – Aqueduct of Valens – Adrianople Gate
"B" – by private car to Old Seraglio, Grand Oriental Bazaars – Old Town.

Athens

"B" – All day excursion by private car to Marathon Battlefield and Cape Sunion.

Venice

"A" – on foot to Doge's Palace – the Dungeons – Bridge of Sighs.
"B" – by gondola to Ca' De Oro – Rialto Bridge – Church of Frari – Church of Santa Maria della Salute.

The late Prime Minister of India, Pandit Nehru, drives the first electric engine to be built at Chittaranjan in 1963.

158

POSTSCRIPT.

Modern expresses electric and diesel hauled.

INDIAN RAILWAYS SINCE 1953.

The first thing that strikes the reader on seeing an Indian Railway Timetable is the plethora of passenger classes. It was announced after Independence that the then four classes would be reduced to two, first and second, with a supplement for Air Conditioned travel on the lines of the supplement for sleeping car accomodation as found in Europe. This however never took place and now there are three Air Conditioned Classes, together with First and Second, the latter being into divided into second class sleeper and ordinary, with different fares charged for Mail or Ordinary trains. In addition, a number of the more important trains charge "special fares" for all classes of passengers.

The actual classes are:

> First Class Air Conditioned ("A" Class), usually referred to as Air Conditioned Class. Two or four berths in compartments.
> Second Class Air Conditioned ("T" Class), 48 berths in two tiers in a semi open coach.
> Air Conditioned Chair Class ("C" Class), reclining chairs.
> First Class ("1"), two, four or six berths in compartments.
> Second Class Sleeper Coach, ("2"), Bunks in an open saloon. Supplement charged.
> Second Class ("2"), seats in an open saloon.

There are no single berth compartments on Indian Railways. A and 1 Class coaches are corridor, but not always vestibuled to the next coach; two lavatories are positioned at each end, of which one only is western (style. An attendent travels in the each coach and is responsible for ordering meals as required, either from the Restaurant Car or from Station Restaurants. Bedding is supplied free to A Class passengers and payment to 1 class.

The population explosion, which occurred in most third world countries, naturally produced a phenomenal rise in India's population, and this is reflected in the number of trains now being run, four or more times greater than before Independence. A typical example is on the Bombay-Delhi route via Ratlam, where originally there were only two fast trains on the Baroda to Delhi section, the Frontier Mail and the Dehra Dun Express. Now there are seven.

Rajdhani Express – A, T, C and restaurant car (RC)
Paschim Express – A, T, 1. 2, and RC.
Frontier Mail – A, T, 1, 2, and RC
Jammu Tawi Express – T, 2.
Dehra Dun Express – 1, 2.
Sarvodaya Express – T, 2.
(unnamed) Express – 2 and RC only

The authorities have named practically every express train, both broad and metre gauge, resulting in literally hundreds of named trains.

This increase of traffic could not have been handled without considerable engineering works to say nothing of the modernisation of signalling and traffic control. The major works have been doubling of main lines and electrification. All main lines serving Delhi, Calcutta, Madras and Bombay haved been doubled; electrification is extensive including Delhi-Calcutta, Delhi-Bombay, by both broad gauge routes, Madras–Bombay and Madras–Calcutta, together with the north–south line from Itarsi to Salem south of Madras. These are probably the longest series of electrified national lines outside of Russia; over 900 miles Calcutta to Delhi and 1640 miles from Delhi to Salem, traversed by the Kerala Express during its journey from Delhi to Trivandrum in the far south.

There have been also three notable river crossings since Independence, two over the Ganges and one over the Brahmaputra, and are part of the improvements to the strategic rail route to Assam; the first bridge was at Mokameh Ghat in Bihar which brought the broad gauge to Barauni on the Lucknow – Gauhati metre gauge line; the second was across the Farrakha Dam near the Bangladesh border. The broad gauge was extended

162

from Barauni to join this line and then continued on, beside or near, to the metre gauge Assam Link to cross the Brahmaputra on a combined broad/metre gauge bridge near Gauhati. The Lucknow-Barauni metre gauge line was also converted so that at the present time it is possible to travel by broad gauge from Lucknow to Gauhati or by metre gauge from Benares via Gauhati to Tinsukia.

It was rashly stated not long after Independence that the metre gauge, comprising over 40% of the total mileage, would be gradually phased out. This has not happened, but a number of lines have been converted. The two most important conversions are the Assam Link, already described, and in the south. These latter conversions consist of a link by passing Madras and the extension of the broad gauge from near Coimbatore to Trivandrum; giving a broad gauge route from Delhi to Trivandrum, without touching Madras.

There is practically no double line anywhere on the metre gauge and only about 95 miles of electrification south of Madras, but important express trains include air conditioned stock and restaurant cars. A curiosity is the Satpura Express on the 2ft 6in gauge line in Madhya Pradesh which boasts an air conditioned "C" class car.

Steam has almost entirely gone from the broad gauge, and it might have gone earlier had it not been for a number of oil crises; India's dependence on Gulf oil has, no doubt, speeded up electrification. The metre gauge has been a paradise for steam locomotive enthusiasts, but it has now been announced that all steam will have gone by 1995.

It might have been thought that the various improvements and modernisation would have brought about a considerable increase in overall speeds, but not so. There is no doubt that the number and length of stops over long distances still conditions speeds. The Rajdhanis, with three or four stops manage about 52 mph overall, well below European standards – even Amtrak, not renowned for speed, produces 58 mph on the Los Angeles-Chicago run of the South West Chief. The Indian "special fare" trains are well below this – the Taj Express with one stop averages 44 mph but the remainder are all in the 36 mph range and some, such as the Frontier and Howrah-Kalka Mails, are still running on almost the identical timings of forty years ago. The metre gauge is much the same – one train in south India averages 28 mph, but the Delhi Mail from Ahmadabad is still on its old timings at 26 mph.

I have tried to make comparisons with neighbouring countries, but this has been difficult owing to differences of distance and number of stops, double or single line and so on. The broad gauge Shalimar Express in Pakistan (Karachi-Lahore) can compare with the Rajdhanis, but the other Mail and Expresses are, like India, running on the timings of forty years ago; Pakistan has an electrified section of about about 180 miles on the Karachi-Lahore line which is entirely on the flat and mostly double.

The metre gauge portion of the Bangladesh Railways between Dacca and Chittagong and the metre gauge Malaysian Railways between Singapore and Kuala Lumpur can clock up overall speeds in the high thirties, but these trains run with few stops for relatively short distances. The other neighbouring metre gauge undertaking, Burma Railways is well below this at 27 mph on the Rangoon-Mandalay line in spite of having what was once alleged to be longest section of double line on the metre gauge in the world, 220 miles.

My wife and I have visited India four times since we left in 1953, but except for one trip on the Frontier Mail, we never travelled on the principal trains, as our itineraries took us away from the tourist track. We missed the old self contained non corridor compartment coaches, although there is no doubt that new corridor stock, with only two doors at each end and an attendant, provides much greater security against thieves. India was, and is, very security conscious, amounting almost to a spy mania, and any foreigner travelling in a way which is thought not to be what a tourist would do immediately falls under suspicion. The inquisitive and bureaucratic Indian mind immediately starts to think "why is this foreigner not on a package tour – why is he not travelling air conditioned, what is he trying to find out!"

164

However a few words of Hindi and the explanation that you are an old Officer, and the atmosphere changes.

In 1974, we had boarded the Bombay through coach at Kanpur en route to Bhopal; we had been staying with my old Regiment who had arranged our tickets and reservations with the (military) Railway Transport Officer (RTO). He had had the tickets endorsed with the train number and date but no berth reservations as ours was a day journey only. The reservation babu arrived and demanded our reservation tickets, getting ruder and more unpleasant by the minute. I explained what had happened and said that the RTO had made the arrangements. This provoked "what has the RTO to do with it, you are not military man." I then let fly in Hindi "you great fool, I served twenty years in the Indian Army, five of them after Independence with Panditji's (Nehru's) Government – how can you say I am not military man". Immediately came the smiles and "but Sir, you are old Officer and you have come all this way to see us, of course all is in order and is there any service that I can do for you?"

1974 was not a good year for us to travel in India. It was just before Mrs Gandhi proclaimed a State of Emergency, and a railway strike was threatened. On this particular journey we arrived at Bhopal on time, but only since no one had pulled the communication cord, a well known form of protest, only to find that our connecting train to Indore had been cancelled, and the next one on the following morning was running twelve hours late – we took a taxi. Earlier we had taken the Dehra Dun-Amritsar Passenger to Jullunder. The up train arrived slightly after our departure time, and the staff flatly refused to leave for the return journey until their turn round time, three hours, had expired. Meanwhile the batteries had gone flat so we had to eat our picnic dinner in almost total darkness. Otherwise, our journeys were as comfortable as our choice of class and train allowed.

By contrast, I had had the good fortune in 1968 to be introduced to a number of senior railway Officers, and this resulted in footplate trips: – Delhi to Tundla, diesel on the Howrah Mail and return, by steam, on the Assam Mail; this locomotive, a

WP, was in first class condition and it was a beautifully smooth ride. A second steam ride was on the Dehra Dun Express from Meerut to Saharanpur; this was on an old worn out AWC 2–8–0 on poor track; sitting on the tender, the jolts were such that I thought I would have broken my back. Later in Bombay, I got footplate rides on the 1500V electric locomotives up the scenic Ghat route to Poona and back. The crew were high in their praise for the few of the Metrovicks still in service, but scathing in their criticism of the imported Chinese models and their opinion of the indigenous built variety was that they were utterly useless.

The last trip I did was on the Kalka Simla, now diesel operated, forty years from when I first travelled on it. Our host in Chandigarh provided a staff car to take me to and from Kalka, so I was able to take the last up train at about 8 am, travel up to Tara Devi, two stations before Simla, where it crossed the first down, transfer to that train, and arrive back at Chandigarh in time for dinner. A memorable trip and a wonderful finale to Indian railway travel.

Metre gauge express still steam hauled.

Darjeeling Mail DHR with new modern rolling stock and original 'B' clan locomotive.

Old and new Bombay suburban motor coaches.

Interior of modern first class compartment coach.

INDEX

Illustrations in BOLD

"A"

ANGLO–INDIANS/BURMESE – 17, 57, 61, 127, 132.

ASSAM, Province of, description – 76.

ASSAM, railways in – Dibru–Sadiya 77, Assam Bengal 77, 78, East Bengal 77, becomes Bengal & Assam Railway 77, effect of floods 79, sabotage 79–83, signalling 81–3.

ASSAM LINK – 130, 132–3

ATTACKS ON PASSENGERS – 135, boy under the seat 135–6.

"B"

BADSHAH Colonel M.M. – 145

BAGHDAD (West) STATION – 44.

BALUCHISTAN, Strategic railways in – history 96–9, Chappar Rift line 98–99, **108, 109**. Bolan Route 98–9, Nushki extension 100, Zhob Valley line 100. Locomotives 100–1.

BARRACKPORE – 87

BASRA – 41

BOMBAY, Ballard Pier – 5

BREWITT Lt Col, Deputy Director of Railways, Burma 57, 59.

BRIDGES, use by Army convoys and tanks – 114.

BRITISH INDIA STEAMSHIPS – SS Dara 139, SS Dwarka 145.

BURMA RAILWAYS – Description 55–6.

"C"

CENTRAL COMMAND, railways in – 111

CHAMAN – 101.

CHIANG KAI-SHEK, Generalissimo – 65–6

CHINESE ARMY, interference with railway operation – 65–8.

CORRUPTION & PILFERING – 87, 90–2, 101–2.

CUFFE, Mr. General Manager B & A Rly – 90.

CURRENCY CONTROL – 146–7, 148, 149.

"D"

DARJEELING–HIMALAYAN RAILWAY – history 127–8, operation 128–9, **140, 141, 142, 168**, locomotives 129, **141**.

DEFENCE OF INDIA UNITS – 88–9.

DIMAPUR (Manipur Road station) – **71.**

"G"

GWYN, Lt Col Philip – 55, 68–9.

"H"

HARDWAR–DEHRA RAILWAY – 24.

HOWRAH (CALCUTTA) STATION, incident with soda wallah – 131.

HUSSAIN Deputy General Manager B & A Rly, Gauhati 82.

HYDAR PASHA (Istanbul) STATION – **152.**

"I"

INCLUSIVE INDIVIDUAL TOUR (Thomas Cook) – 143–4, & Appendix.

INDIAN RAILWAYS – history 11–2, train services 12, rolling stock 5, **6**, 7, 13. air conditioning 13–4, signalling 16, **16, 85**. Staff 17, bridges **17, 19, 84, 122–2**.

171

After Independence – reconstruction of GIP Ghat lines 133, train services 133, reorganisation 133–4.

Present day – passenger classes 161, modernisation and electrification 162–3, **160, 169, 170,** comparison of speeds 163–4.

IRAQ RAILWAYS – description 41–2, train services 42–3, repatriation of Axis Nationals 49–50.

"J"

JODHPUR RAILWAY – 31–2

JOHNSTON "Two Gin", Captain SS Dara – 139

"K"

KALKA–SIMLA RAILWAY – 22–4, **32–6,** 136.

KHYBER RAILWAY – 30, **34.**

"L"

LOCOMOTIVE TYPES, Indian, *Broad Gauge* – "HP" 7, 14, 31, 119, 127, "HG" 14, 101, 119, "E1(E/M)" **8,** 9, 14, 31, "SP" 9, 14, 31, "SG" 9, **10,** 15, "XA" 15, 101, "XB" 15, "XC" **8,** 15, **17, 19,** 31, "L" 100, **105,** "N" 101, **106,** "Mallet" 101, **106,** "XG (XG/M)" 101, **107,** "AWC", "AWD", "CWD", "AWE" 112, "CWC" 120, "WP" 132 **139,** "WG" 132, Electric 17, **19.**
Metre Gauge – "YB" 15, 29, 126, "H" 31.**36,** 126, modern **167**
Narrow Gauge – (KS Rly) "K" 23, **32, 33,** (Zhob Valley) "G" **107** 103, (DHR) "B" 129 141 "Garratt" 129.
Middle East – Iraq, metre gauge, "H" Class 42, standard gauge, "Borsig" 43, . Turkey 48, **51.**

LUCKNOW STATION – **84.**

"M"

MACK, Driver Mhow Shed – 131–2.

MADRAS & SOUTHERN MAHRATTA RAILWAY – 29.

MAINS, Lt Col A.A. – schoolboy journeys xiii, xiv, choice of career xiv, commissioned and sails to India 3, first Indian Journey 5 *et seq*, troop train to the Simla Hills 21–2, leave to England 1935 24–5, troop train to Nowshera 29–30, travels from Peshawar to Karachi via Bombay 31–2, becomes Head of Security, Iraq Force 41, visits Syria by train 47–8, Taurus Express stoned by Bedouin 48–9 becomes Head of Security Burma Army 55, rail tour interrupted by Japanese bombing 62–3, arrives back in India, journey from Assam to Delhi 68–70, admitted to New Delhi Hospital 70, appointed Head of Security in (Assam 73, journey from Dehra Dun to Gauhati 74–76, tours Assam in Officer's saloon 83–86, becomes Head of Security of XIV Army 87, troop train Barrackpore to Comilla 87, posted to 5/9th Gurkha Rifles in Baluchistan 95, journey from Comilla to Chaman 95–6, roundabout journey Kalyan to Wana on return from home leave 104–5, journey from Wana to Agra 111, becomes Chief Intelligence Officer Central Command 111, two unfortunate journeys 136–7, footplate rides in 1968 165–6.

MAINS, Lt Col & Mrs P.M. – Mrs Mains first Indian journey 114–5, journey to Quetta 115, return to India on "Staff College Special" 117–22, journey to Mhow 125, leave to Darjeeling 126–7, return 130–132, leave to Aleppo and Beirut 137–9. return to England with baby daughter overland from Basra 143–52 & Appendix, journeys in 1974 164–5.

172

MORALE, railway staff – 81–2, 88, 132.

MANDALAY STATION, destroyed by Japanese bombs 63–65, **71.**

"N"

NAMED TRAINS, India – Imperial Indian Mail 5, Frontier Mail 5, 7, 9, 32, Karachi Mail **19,** 95, (GIP) Punjab Mail **18,** 27–8, 111, 115, Deccan Queen 28, Gujerat Mail 31, Delhi Mail (metre gauge) 31, Bolan Mail 32, 95 . Assam Mail 70, Toofan Express 70, Doon Express 74, 95, Surma Mail (metre gauge) 74–5, (EIR) Punjab Mail 95, 112, Quetta Passenger (96, **109,** 115, Grand Trunk Express 112, 114, (GIP) Calcutta Mail 126, Darjeeling Mail 127.

Middle East – Taurus Express 43–4, 138, 146–7, **50, 152** Baghdad Mail (metre gauge) 42.

Europe – P & O Express 25–27, Simplon Orient 149–50 **153,** Golden Arrow 150, Direct Orient, Tauern Orient, Athens & Marmora Expresses 151.

NEVASA Troopship – 3, **4.**

"P"

PARTITION DISTURBANCES – 116.

PASSPORT CONTROL, Taurus Express – 45–6.

"R"

RAILCARS. KS Railway – 23–4, **33, 36.**

RAJPUTANA MALWA RAILWAY – 125–6.

RANGOON STATION, Evacuation trains 57–61, Rangoon Police try to storm station 60–1.

RIVER STEAMERS, 74–5.

"S"

SIND SAGAR DOAB RAILWAY – 105.

SIRCAR, Mr, Deputy Chief Commercial Manager EIR – 130–1

SPECIAL MILITARY EXPRESSES – 104, 115.

STAFF COLLEGE SPECIAL – 116–22.

STRIKES – 113.

SYRIAN RAILWAYS – Description 47–8.

"T"

TUNNELS – Parsnik **85,** Shelabagh 98, 102

"U"

U.S. ARMY – lack of discipline 86, take over operation of Assam Railways 89–90.

"W"

WAGG, Alfred, War Correspondent – 69–70.

"Z"

ZHOB VALLEY LINE journeys – in a blizzard 102–4, floods 104.